PRAISE FOR *WASTED PRAYER*

For years, I've helped people figure out what they should do with their lives. One of the biggest roadblocks is the fear of moving forward when you should be waiting on God. I'm extremely thankful that my friend and fellow thought leader Greg took on this challenge in this great book!

—JON ACUFF, *NEW YORK TIMES* BEST-SELLING
AUTHOR OF *START* AND *STUFF CHRISTIANS LIKE*

Greg Darley has spent his life in pursuit of the things that matter most. This book is a manifesto for making your one precious life count.

—BEN ARMENT, CREATOR OF STORY

Greg says, "The key is to stop praying and start doing." I told Greg when he pitched this book concept to me that he'd get pushback at the concept, but then I told him I wish I had written this book, and I'm glad he did. It's needed. I've watched so many times as the church I pastor "prays" about something so long that we actually miss the opportunities God was bringing our way. Looking back, I wish we had done what we already knew in our hearts we should have been doing. The same is true in my personal life. This book will challenge and inspire you. And, you won't stop praying, You'll probably even pray more. But, you'll pray better prayers—and do better and more Kingdom work.

—RON EDMONDSON, PASTOR, IMMANUEL BAPTIST CHURCH

Wasted Prayer is a fresh call for Christians to pursue the dreams and visions that God gives. It will help you not o̶n̶... ...ayer but the entire way in which y...

—ROD STAFFORD, SENIOR ... ...RCH

Greg Darley's new book *Wasted Prayer* disturbs the part of me that wants distinct clarity before taking action. Yet time and time again God doesn't provide the blue prints, he simply provides the next step. Greg's advice to "Stop praying. Start doing." is both terrifying and liberating and will challenge you to hear from God in a new way.

—JENNI CATRON, CHURCH LEADER AND AUTHOR OF *CLOUT: DISCOVER AND UNLEASH YOUR GOD-GIVEN INFLUENCE*

Greg is one of the brightest young leaders I know. He combines a passionate heart with a thoughtful approach to solving problems and helping people. Many people talk about trying to change the world. Greg's out doing that, today.

—JEFF HENDERSON, LEAD PASTOR, GWINNETT CHURCH

WASTED PRAYER

WASTED PRAYER

KNOW WHEN GOD WANTS YOU TO STOP PRAYING AND START DOING

GREG DARLEY

NELSON
BOOKS

An Imprint of Thomas Nelson

Published in Nashville, Tennessee, by Nelson Books, an imprint of Thomas Nelson. Nelson Books and Thomas Nelson are registered trademarks of HarperCollins Christian Publishing, Inc.

Author is represented by the literary agency of Mark Sweeney & Associates, 28540 Altessa Way, Suite 201, Bonita Springs, FL 34135.

Thomas Nelson, Inc., titles may be purchased in bulk for educational, business, fund-raising, or sales promotional use. For information, please e-mail SpecialMarkets@ThomasNelson.com.

Unless otherwise indicated, Scripture quotations are taken from the *Holy Bible, New International Version*®, NIV®. Copyright © 1973, 1978, 1984, 2011 by Biblica, Inc.™ Used by permission of Zondervan. All rights reserved worldwide. www.zondervan.com

ISBN: 978-1-40020-644-5

Library of Congress Control Number: 2013958090

Printed in the United States of America

14 15 16 17 18 RRD 6 5 4 3 2 1

*To my children: I know God has big plans for your lives!
I can't wait to see all you accomplish. I love you so much!*

CONTENTS

CONTENTS

PART TWO: START DOING

FOREWORD
BY MARK BATTERSON

PRAYER IS ONE OF THE OLDEST AND MOST SACRED PRACTICES of Christianity. For thousands of years, people have been praying to God, seeking his guidance, and looking for answers. Some prayers come during high religious services and others while running through the airport, desperate to make a connecting flight.

Because I'm a pastor, prayer plays a large role in my life. I say prayers in churches, during ceremonies, before meals, and at home with my family. I pray in staff meetings, on retreats, and before I preach. I pray with church members who are hurting. I pray as I write books and prepare sermons. I spend time in prayer walking through neighborhoods in DC where we live and minister.

A few years ago, during one of these prayer walks, I saw some property that I thought would be perfect for our church. Finding affordable commercial property in Washington, DC, usually takes a miracle for a business, much less a church. We wanted a place where we could serve the community and have a place to host our Sunday morning worship gatherings.

So I did what most pastors would have done: I prayed. I prayed that we could get the property, reminding God of all the good we could do if it belonged to the church instead of some business. I prayed that we would find favor with the seller and the zoning commission. I prayed that a miracle would happen.

Would anyone object to this behavior? Of course not. Prayer is woven into the DNA of Christianity and the Bible. Prayer is foundational to our relationship with God. It's something every follower of Jesus should be doing every day.

But sometimes prayer can be an obstacle in the very relationship it is trying to build. This is why I am so excited about the message of this book. In *Wasted Prayer,* my friend Greg Darley shines a light on the truth that sometimes saying prayers falls short of what God wants us to do. There are times when only action can accomplish the miracle that we desire.

In praying for the miracle property, I learned that there were many steps I needed to take if we even wanted a chance at getting the property, much less actually buying it. There were calls to make, forms to fill out, and meetings to attend. In short, if all I had done was pray about the property, I would not have seen God unfold one of the greatest miracles of my life, and we wouldn't be holding services there every week. There is a time to pray and a time to act. I hope you will enjoy the challenge of this book as much as I did.

INTRODUCTION

WHAT IS YOUR REACTION WHEN YOU HEAR THAT A FRIEND IS selling his or her business to become a missionary on the other side of the world? How do you feel when you learn that a neighbor nearing retirement has adopted a teenager out of the foster care system? What do you think when you hear that your siblings have forgiven your father for walking out on the family decades ago?

When I hear stories like these, my first thought is always one of awe. *Wow,* I think. *That is incredible. How in the world could they do that? I'm not sure I could.* Maybe you would think something like, *That person must have incredible faith.* Incredible faith indeed. It takes incredible faith to sell the lucrative law firm to become a missionary. It takes incredible faith to adopt a teenager in your fifties. It takes incredible faith to offer forgiveness to those who have hurt us deeply. But where does that incredible faith come from? How do you get to the place where you are even willing to sell your business, much less actually do it?

My purpose in writing is to dig into the heart of all these questions. The life of faith is one of adventure and excitement. It is also one of fear and uncertainty. The key is to find a way around the fear and seize the adventure God desires for your life. The key is to stop praying and start doing.

PART ONE

STOP PRAYING

CHAPTER 1

JUMP!

"IF YOU JUMP, I PROMISE I'LL CATCH YOU," MY BROTHER SAID to his son last summer at the pool. At age four, jumping off the three-foot diving board into the deep end was a big deal.

"Dad, I'm scared," Parker said.

His legs were trembling as he looked down into the deep water. He had never been allowed to swim over there by himself. The shake in his voice revealed that this was his first time jumping off the diving board.

"I'm right here, son," my brother reassured him. "It's okay. Just jump."

All the family was watching, but there was no jump.

"Do you want to jump?" my brother asked.

Parker nodded his head, but still he didn't jump.

"You know I will catch you, right?"

Again, Parker nodded.

However, a few seconds went by and he was still standing there, not moving, just buying time. He's not that different from you and me, really. This is a good picture of what most of our spiritual lives look like. When God tells us to jump, our reactions are the same as my nephew's. We tell God we *want* to jump. We even tell God we *will* jump. But we don't. We stand there, frozen in time. When someone asks us why we haven't jumped yet, we often respond with, "I'm praying about it."

And at that point, the case is closed, because no one is going to get on your back for praying. Of course you should pray. That's what God wants, right?

I don't think so. And that's the premise of this book.

The best thing you can do to start living the life God wants for you is to stop just praying. Is your level of joy nonexistent? Are you frustrated with the level of your faith? Stop praying. If your marriage is struggling or your relationship with your kids is poor, stop praying. Do you find anger, jealousy, or fear ruining every week? Then stop praying. If you are in a financial black hole—stop praying.

In fact, I think God wants you to stop praying about all these issues. *God wants me to stop praying?* Yes, you read that correctly. Clearly not what you would expect from a Christian book, I know; but hear me out.

There's a second part to this directive: *start doing.* That's when you start doing what God has called you to do. Sometimes prayer is not enough. God wants you to stop praying about whether you should obey what he's called you to do and just start obeying. He wants you to stop praying about your marriage and start living out your relationship the way he's commanded. He wants you to stop praying about your credit card debt and start handling your money the way he's instructed you to. He wants you to stop praying about your fear and start doing what he's called you to do.

God really wants you to stop praying and start doing. If Martin Luther King Jr. had *only* prayed about leading nonviolent protest, would the civil rights movement have succeeded? When would slaves have been set free if Abraham Lincoln had *only* prayed about delivering the Emancipation Proclamation? How many people would have missed hearing the gospel if Billy Graham had *only* prayed about starting a ministry? What if your parents had *only* prayed about having you? Prayer is important, but sometimes it stands in the way of what God wants you to do.

Before you write me off as a heretic and burn this book, let me clarify a few points. God doesn't want you to stop praying about everything. Just some things. Prayer is good, except when it stops you from doing what God has called you to do. Then prayer is bad. In fact, prayer can be detrimental. Don't believe me? Well, read on.

GET OFF THE GROUND

A common theme in the Old Testament is that the Israelites won when God went with the army and blessed them. If God was fighting for them, no one could resist their force. They would sweep the enemies unscathed. But the opposite was also true. When God wasn't with them, even the smallest competitor could stand against them. God promised Joshua that if the Israelites would obey his commands and serve him only, God would rout all their enemies.

After decades of marching through the desert, the Israelites finally crossed over the Jordan River on their way to the promised land. The only problem was, the promised land was filled with other people's cities, tribes, and armies. The fulfillment of the promised land would only be experienced through war.

The first city they approached was Jericho, and the men were itching for battle. They'd been waiting for this day a long time. Joshua gave them simple directions: "Once God brings the walls down, destroy every living thing. Do not keep any devoted items for yourselves, for these belong in the Lord's treasury" (Josh. 6:18–19, paraphrased).

Now, Jericho was a well-fortified city, but God was with the Israelites, so they completely conquered Jericho and all its people. So far, so good. Next was a smaller town named Ai. Joshua sent men to spy on the city and develop a battle plan. When they returned to Joshua, they said, "Not all the army will have to go up against Ai. Send two or three thousand men to take it and do not weary the whole army, for only a few people live there" (Josh. 7:3).

The spies sized up the inhabitants of Ai and compared them to the people of Jericho, whom they had just wiped out. There was no way Ai had a chance. This was like an NFL team playing a high school team. It was not possible they could lose. So Joshua decided to give most of the men the day off and sent a small force.

So about three thousand went up; but they were routed by the men of Ai, who killed about thirty-six of them. They chased the Israelites from the city gate as far as the stone quarries and struck them down on the slopes. At this the hearts of the people melted in fear and became like water. (Josh. 7:4–5)

What must Joshua have been feeling as he looked up and saw his men running toward the camp, being pursued and cut down by the inferior troops of Ai? This must have been incredibly frightening for him and all the Israelites. What was God doing? They had just destroyed the fortified city of Jericho, but now the little town of Ai repelled their forces, beating them with ease.

Suffering an embarrassing defeat would drive most people to prayer. Clearly, Joshua thought this was a time to pray too. "Then Joshua tore his clothes and fell facedown to the ground before the ark of the LORD, remaining there till evening. The elders of Israel did the same, and sprinkled dust on their heads" (Josh. 7:6).

Joshua went on to ask God why he even brought them over the Jordan if they were to be destroyed by small towns like Ai. Further, he asked God what would happen to God's name in the region once word spread that the Israelites had been beaten.

God's response was not quite what Joshua was expecting. Bluntly, God said, "Stand up! What are you doing down on your face?" (Josh. 7:10).

God wanted to know why Joshua was praying. Joshua assumed, as most of us do, that we should pray when things go wrong. In our times of need, prayer is the logical option. If the Israelites didn't win the battle, the obvious next step was prayer. Or so Joshua thought.

But God didn't want Joshua to pray. "Get off the ground. This is not the time to pray; this is the time to act!" That was essentially God's response.

> What are you doing down on your face? Israel has sinned; they have violated my covenant, which I commanded them to keep. They have taken some of the devoted things; they have stolen, they have lied, they have put them with their own possessions. That is why the Israelites cannot stand against their enemies; they turn their backs and run because they have been made liable to destruction. I will not be with you anymore unless you destroy whatever among you is devoted to destruction. (Josh. 7:10–12)

God told Joshua that Israel was losing because they were being disobedient, and the only way to fix the situation wasn't to pray—it was to act. God didn't want Joshua or any Israelite just praying; he wanted them acting. God reminded Joshua that no Israelite was supposed to take any devoted thing from Jericho, including gold, silver, or fine clothing. It was obvious that someone had been disobedient. Prayer could not help Joshua's situation. This was what I call a wasted prayer. When we pray about following a command God has given us, it is a wasted prayer. When we pray about following a command God has given us, it is a wasted prayer. Joshua was busy praying when God had given him a clear call. Joshua was praying a wasted prayer.

The next day, Joshua had each tribe stand before him to see who had taken the devoted things. Achan, from the tribe of Judah, came forward and admitted he had taken gold, silver, and a beautiful robe and hid them under his tent. Joshua had Achan's tent searched. They found the plunder just as Achan had admitted. The devoted things, along with Achan's family and everything he owned, were taken outside the camp to be stoned and burned. After this was finished, the Israelites were able to wipe out Ai and completely destroy the city.

I know the end of that story isn't the typical fairy-tale ending, but that's not the point. The point is that God values obedience over religious acts, including prayer. Further, if we do turn to prayer in situations like this, it is important to know that God wants us to get off the ground, stop praying, and start doing!

Here's another point: God doesn't want you to do just anything. He wants you to do what he's called you to do. Some of these callings will be the same for all followers of Christ, but others are specifically for you. If you aren't living the type of life you desire, it may be time for you to stop praying and start doing.

Who doesn't want to live a more exciting life? Who wouldn't want to be more obedient to what God has called him or her to? My goal is to convince you to stop praying, but not completely. I'm referring to the misuse of certain prayers at certain times. Sometimes we willingly misuse prayer, knowingly and on purpose. Other times we have no idea our prayers have become an obstacle for us to be obedient to God's call. The first section of this book focuses on specific misuses of prayer and how we can avoid them. Later, we will look at how we can counteract the misuses and start following through on what God has called us to do.

CHAPTER 2

GET MOVING

THE STORY OF ABRAHAM STARTS OUT AT AN ALARMINGLY FAST pace. It's like watching the first hour of a two-hour movie in fast-forward with little explanation at all. We're given a few verses about Abraham's family, whom he married, and where they lived. That's it. We know he was a herdsman and probably pretty wealthy. He had gained enough assets to be able to move when and where he wanted. We don't know what his personality was like. We don't know if he was a hard worker or what kind of sense of humor he had. We don't know his hair color or his favorite food. And we don't know what his prayer life was like.

This is how the author of Genesis introduces the story of Abraham: "The LORD had said to Abram [later named Abraham], 'Go from your country, your people and your father's household to the land I will show you'" (Gen. 12:1).

In the very first scene of the story, Abraham is told to pack up everything he owns and set out to a destination yet to be determined. He is to leave the familiarity of home. He is to leave the comfort of family. He is to leave the support of his father's household. He is to leave the financial support of his job. He is not told where to go, only that he *is* to go. This is no small request. Imagine what that conversation was like with his wife, Sarai:

"Sarai, honey, you need to pack my suitcase and load up the two-humped camel."

"What are you talking about, Abram?" she asks.

"God told me to move."

"Where?"

"I'm not certain," he tells her.

"What do you mean, you don't know?"

"Well, that's the truth. I don't really know. God just said to move."

"When is this move supposed to take place?" she asks.

"Right now."

"So, you're going to leave your home, your family, all your friends, the comfort of this land, and head off to a place yet to be determined, without a map, without knowing if it will be a good place to raise a family?"

"Uhhh . . . I know it sounds crazy. But yes. That's exactly the plan."

If you have a moment like this, I would implore you to take more than three minutes to discuss this decision with your spouse. Since we don't know how that conversation went between Abram and Sarai, I'll just assume some artistic freedom that it went along those lines.

The good news for Abram was that God added a little incentive to the deal:

I will make you into a great nation, and I will bless you; I will make your name great, and you will be a blessing. I will bless those who bless you, and whoever curses you I will curse; and all peoples on earth will be blessed through you. (Gen. 12:2–3)

At least he was able to share some good news with Sarai.

"But if we go," he tells her, "God said he'd make our family into a great nation."

"What do you mean 'nation'?" she asks.

"I assume he means a lot of people. How else would all the peoples of the earth be blessed through me?"

This seems to be the offer of a lifetime. We find out later how badly they wanted children. It finally sounds as if they'll get their wish. It's like the Palestine Powerball. Abram had just won the lottery. All he had to do to cash in the winning ticket was pack up and go.

If you were Abram, what would you do? This isn't really a fair question because you know the end of the story, but pretend you only had the limited information Abram had. What would be the very first thing you'd do? If you were sitting in a Sunday school class, you would feel very confident in saying, "Pray!" Of course you would. It's what we would all do.

But not Abram.

After God finished talking, the narrator tells us, "So Abram went, as the Lord had told him" (Gen. 12:4). That was it. He didn't call for a family prayer meeting. There was no fasting and meditating to decide what to do. There wasn't any hesitation. God spoke; Abram acted.

Now, you're probably saying, "But that's different. You don't know my situation. Besides, God told Abraham he was going to bless him and make him into a great nation. Who wouldn't obey after that promise?"

You're right. I don't know you or your situation. And yes, Abraham had some incentive. But is that incentive really any different today? I don't think it is.

Sure, on some technical grounds, the incentive of being made into a great nation is different than the promises God has given us. But not as different as we may assume. The real issue is whether or not we believe that what God has called us to do is ultimately in our best interests. Do we believe that following God is better than not following him? We all want to believe that's true. But in this instance, what we do trumps what we believe. Our beliefs will be confirmed by our actions. If we really believe that God has something better for us, we will pack up and move—just like Abraham—when God tells us to.

WALK OF SHAME

Wasted prayers have stopped many people from living the life God called them to live. Sometimes prayer leaves us with regret, because we look back and realize that we spent our time praying instead of acting. Instead of having memories of God acting on our behalf, of our faith being stretched, of ourselves doing things for God we didn't think were possible, we have feelings of regret because we sat scared on the sidelines.

We have no stories to share about obvious movements when God acted in our lives. Instead of acting, we were praying.

The summer between my junior and senior years of high school, two of my best friends, Adam and Tyler, and I spent a few days hanging out at Tyler's lake house in the mountains of northern Georgia. We did all the typical lake activities like swimming, riding the Jet Ski, waterskiing, wakeboarding, and inner tubing. Inner tubing was the best. We'd pull two people on different tubes and have an all-out brawl to see who could stay on the longest. There were no rules. It was every man for himself. The trick was to kick the other person's tube in a downward motion as he was coming off the wake with some momentum. When in doubt, it was always fun to jump off your tube onto the other guy's and try to throw him off à la Jack Sparrow.

After a long day of playing on the water, the three of us, along with Tyler's parents, were cruising back to the house in the boat. We slowed down to pass under a bridge and saw some people jumping off into the water. It looked like a lot of fun. When I was younger, my brother and I used to go bridge jumping on the lake where my grandparents had a house.

"I've done that before," I proudly told everyone. A few eyebrows raised.

"Why don't you boys go jump then?" Tyler's mom asked.

The three of us looked at one another. No one said anything.

"I'll pull the boat closer to the shore so you won't have to swim as far," his dad said. He'd decided for us.

All three of us jumped out of the boat and swam to shore. The shore was lined with big rocks, so climbing out of the water and making our way to the road wasn't fun. We climbed barefoot over rocks, through weeds, pine needles, and gravel. When we got to the top, we marched back down the road to the center of the bridge, finding the jump-off point above the deepest water. I put my hands on the wall and leaned over to get a good look at the water.

"That sure does look a lot higher from up here!" I said to my friends.

"Seriously!" one said back.

Leaning against the concrete ledge, I took a deep breath. There was no way to jump from where we were standing. You had to step up on the edge of the wall so you didn't risk tripping and doing a face-plant over the bridge. We all spread out and stepped up onto the ledge.

I have never been a big fan of heights. My knees started to get weak. Looking down at the water, my heart pounded. *What in the world am I doing up here?* I took a deep breath and knew that I couldn't do it. Looking over to my friends, their faces said the same thing.

"I think I'm going back down," I said.

"Me too."

"I'll go too."

And we all stepped down from the ledge, retracing our steps across the hot concrete, through the woods, over the pine needles, rocks, and weeds, finally wading into the water and swimming back to the boat.

Looking back, I have nothing but regret and shame. If I wasn't able to use this experience as an illustration, I would never share it. I regret not jumping. I regret being a coward. Because jumping makes a much better story than dropping my head and walking back down. If I had jumped, I would have had an incredible memory to look back on. Instead, I only have a story of embarrassment. I think most of the regrets we'll have at the end of our lives will be for the opportunities we didn't seize rather than the mistakes we've made.

SECOND CHANCES

I'm thankful for second chances, and that my bridge-jumping story has redemption in the end. The month after graduating high school, the same friends and I were back at the lake. This time, however, we were with a group of friends, and we'd had a whole year to regret not jumping. After spending the day out on the water again, we found ourselves staring at the same bridge, also known as our nemesis.

As the boat slowed down, a friend who hadn't been there the previous summer suggested we all go and jump. My two other friends on Team Don't Jump looked at each other as if to say, *Oh no. There's no way we're doing that again*. But with more friends present this time, we decided we had to do it. The boat slowed down, and people started jumping into the water. I found myself doing the same. A few friends, though, decided to hang back in the safety of the boat.

So there I was again, swimming to the same shore, climbing the same rocks, walking back down the same road, facing our nemesis from the previous summer. But this time was different. I'd had an entire year to think about this moment. I knew my problem was that I had waited until I stood on the ledge to make my decision to jump. This time, I made up my mind that I was jumping no matter what. I wasn't going to wait until the moment I stared down at the water.

As I approached the center of the bridge, a friend was already there, waiting for us to catch up.

"Is it all clear below?" I asked.

He looked over the edge. "Yeah, it's clear."

I walked right up to him, stood up on the ledge, and without pausing, I jumped!

"Ahhh!" *Splash!*

It lasted for maybe a few seconds. My heart was pounding. I looked up at all my friends peering over the edge and yelled, "Come on! What are you waiting for?"

One by one, they all eventually jumped. After everyone made his or her initial leap, we decided to jump again—this time all at once, and we would get Tyler's mom to snap a picture from the boat. We all swam back to shore, climbed the rocks, walked up the road, and climbed onto the ledge eight feet apart from one another.

"We all have to go on three," a friend yelled.

Everyone agreed.

"One!"

Everyone looked down, then right and left.

"Two!"

It was a lot easier to just jump without standing on the ledge so long.

"Three!"

In unison, all nine of us jumped. Once we hit the water and came up for air, we were yelling excitedly. We'd all jumped.

With almost perfect irony, Tyler's mom yelled from the boat that the picture didn't take. So, for a fourth time, I made the swim to the shore, climbed the rocks, walked up the road, and all nine of us made the jump again. And now we had the picture to prove it.

That makes for a much better story. I've had a copy of that picture in my office for more than ten years. I'm glad the nine of us jumped. I know the others are glad too. I wonder, though, if my two friends who stayed in the boat the entire time ever regret not jumping. I wonder if they even remember that moment.

That's what it looks like when we don't do what God calls us to do. We sit around in the boat while others are making picture-worthy memories. I learned that the shame and guilt of not acting was worse than the initial fear.

I know that a juvenile story from high school isn't the same as your situation, but perhaps it's not so different. You have a bridge, and God is calling you to jump off it. It could be accepting a new job, starting a new relationship, ending a bad relationship, changing degrees, planting a church, selling your business, going back to school, having children, adopting, downsizing your home . . . the possibilities are endless.

There are two things I know to be true about your situation:

1. If you don't jump, you are being disobedient to God.
2. If you don't jump, you will eventually regret it. You will

look back, as I did, and wish you had jumped off the bridge. And unfortunately, you're not guaranteed a second chance.

WHAT "DOING" IS *NOT* ABOUT

Before we go any further, let's clarify some terms so that we're all using the same language. A red flag goes up for many people when anything relating to the idea of "works" comes into the conversation. As it is referred to in Ephesians 2:8–9, *works* (or "doing") are often seen to be opponents to the gospel of grace. "For it is by grace you have been saved, through faith—and this is not from yourselves, it is the gift of God—not by works, so that no one can boast." If we talk about works, people may assume they can earn their way to God. This is dangerous, so let me clarify a few points.

First, doing what God has called you to do isn't about earning your way to God. Salvation is not earned; it's a gift from God. Salvation is only possible by his grace, and it always will be. Doing something for God is always a response to his grace, never an attempt to buy or earn it.

Consider the following verses:

> But because of his great love for us, God, who is rich in mercy, made us alive with Christ even when we were dead in transgressions—it is by grace you have been saved. (Eph. 2:4–5)

Now to the one who works, wages are not credited as a gift but as an obligation. However, to the one who does not work but trusts God who justifies the ungodly, their faith is credited as righteousness. (Rom. 4:4–5)

When Simon saw that the Spirit was given at the laying on of the apostles' hands, he offered them money and said, "Give me also this ability so that everyone on whom I lay my hands may receive the Holy Spirit."

Peter answered: "May your money perish with you, because you thought you could buy the gift of God with money!" (Acts 8:18–20)

I'm assuming that the principles in this book are for those who have already placed their faith in Christ. "Doing," as I'm referring to it, has nothing to do with salvation. I am in no way saying that we can earn our salvation through works. This is not a book on salvation. This is a book on becoming obedient disciples of Jesus Christ. And I believe that will happen when you stop praying and start doing.

CHAPTER 3

PRAY CONTINUALLY?

IN 1 THESSALONIANS, PAUL WRITES TO A GROUP OF BELIEV-
ers and gives them this instruction: "Rejoice always, pray
continually, give thanks in all circumstances; for this is God's
will for you in Christ Jesus" (5:16–18).

At first glance, it seems that the commands to stop praying and pray continually are inconsistent. But I am convinced
that they are not in opposition at all, but rather are working
together.

REACTIONARY PRAYERS

Most of us define prayer in a few ways:

1. Prayer is a way to ask God for something we want. *Lord,
   I need a new job, or for the house to sell, or for the kids to
   get into a certain school.*

2. Prayer is a way to ask God for things to change. *Lord, please heal my sick friend, save my dying parent, or help change my disobedient child.*
3. Prayer is a way to figure out what to do. *Lord, should I go to this school, take that job, or marry this person?*
4. Prayer is a way to thank God. *Lord, thank you for this meal we are about to receive.*

Most people's prayer lives mainly consist of what I call reactionary prayers. We go through life until something unexpected happens—for example, a friend gets sick or a spouse is laid off from work. When this happens, we pray. It doesn't have to be negative events like sickness or death either. Perhaps you are accepted into multiple schools. Which one should you attend? You may get a job offer that would require you to relocate your family. Should you go?

In all these situations, our prayers are mainly reactions to the events in our lives. We pray for God to act on our behalf in light of these actions. These are reactionary prayers. Reactionary prayers are a normal part of faith and life. I'm not condemning someone for praying when he or she is laid off from work or when a friend falls sick. That should be expected. But if our prayers are only reactionary, we will not only have a difficult time making the best decision but we'll also miss one of the main benefits of prayer.

The story of Abraham is compelling to me because God turned Abraham's life upside down with a request to move to a region he probably considered to be the other side of the world. If ever there was an opportunity for a reactionary prayer, that was it. But Abraham didn't pray. He packed up and moved. I marvel at this. For Abraham, this wasn't an opportunity to react in prayer; this was an opportunity to engage in a relationship.

THE ALTERNATIVE

The opposite of reactive is proactive, and this is the key. If we can shift our prayer lives toward proactivity rather than re-activity, we will greatly increase our ability to hear from God. Then we can stop praying and start doing. The difference in being proactive is that we pray and converse with God long before he calls or an event throws us into confusion. The lon-ger we are proactive in our prayers, the easier those decisions become. A proactive prayer life is more about a relationship than a transaction. A reactive prayer life is trying to get the most out of a transaction; the answer is the ultimate goal. Once the answer is given, the reactive pray-er goes on with life until another disaster strikes.

As one's proactive prayer life increases, so does the intimacy of one's relationship with the Father. Such a person says prayers constantly and consistently before any event, strengthening the trust between that person and God. Then when a potentially life-altering event happens, he or she is better equipped to make the right decision.

But it doesn't stop there. The proactive pray-er's desire is intimacy with the Father; so when God calls, the proactive pray-er wants to act. Because the relationship is deep and con-sistent, the person is confident enough to stop praying about whether or not he or she *should* do something, and instead step out in faith and do it. The goal then is to pray continually before any event occurs, so that your focus is on the relationship and not the transaction.

PAUL'S PRAYER LIFE

We see from Paul's life that he was a proactive pray-er. He didn't just pray in response to events in his life; rather, prayer was a consistent part of his daily routine. Consider the following example:

One day, Paul and Silas were ministering in the city of Philippi. Paul led times of prayer and worship outside the city gate, near the river. On one such occasion, while walking to his place of prayer, he encountered a slave girl who was demon-possessed. We will consider this "an event."

Before we move on with the story, notice that Paul was on his way to spend time in prayer before the event occurred. Paul had been spending time conversing with God in prayer and devotion. The gospel was fresh on his heart. He was focused on his relationship with Jesus.

And then the demon-possessed slave walked by. Luke, the writer of Acts, wrote that the slave predicted the future, which earned a great deal of money for her owners. Luke explained:

> She followed Paul and the rest of us, shouting, "These men are servants of the Most High God, who are telling you the way to be saved." She kept this up for many days. Finally

Paul became so annoyed that he turned around and said to the spirit, "In the name of Jesus Christ I command you to come out of her!" At that moment the spirit left her. (Acts 16:17–18)

When Paul cast the demon from the slave girl, he wasn't reacting solely to her following him around and shouting behind him what he was doing and whom he worked for. That would have been strange for anyone. Just imagine a person walking behind you yelling, "This is Tom. He works for Smith Accounting. He's telling you how to save money on your taxes!" If she had been doing this for many days at your office, you'd want to shut her up too.

But Paul wasn't simply trying to shut her up. Before he encountered her, he had been spending time in prayer. I believe that Paul helped this girl because he was so focused on Jesus and the gospel that he was distraught at her bondage. The gospel frees people, and Paul had to help her.

So Paul didn't just react to a random event in his life. He was proactive in his relationship with the Father and didn't have to pray about whether or not he should help the girl.

But this event was only the beginning. It set in motion a trail of events that many would consider misfortune. Had Paul really done the right thing? Luke continued:

When her owners realized that their hope of making money was gone, they seized Paul and Silas and dragged them into the marketplace to face the authorities. They brought them before the magistrates and said, "These men are Jews, and are throwing our city into an uproar by advocating customs unlawful for us Romans to accept or practice."

The crowd joined in the attack against Paul and Silas, and the magistrates ordered them to be stripped and beaten with rods. After they had been severely flogged, they were thrown into prison, and the jailer was commanded to guard them carefully. When he received these orders, he put them in the inner cell and fastened their feet in the stocks. (Acts 16:19–24)

At this point, surely Paul was thinking that he'd made a mistake in healing the girl. I know I would have questioned God about being beaten for helping someone. But Paul didn't question God. Because of his proactive prayer life, we see that Paul had quite the opposite reaction: "About midnight Paul and Silas were praying and singing hymns to God, and the other prisoners were listening to them" (Acts 16:25).

So Paul was praying before the event and after the consequences of his obedience during that event. But we'd all be praying if we'd just been wrongfully accused and thrown into prison, right? We'd be praying, *God, get us the heck out of here. We didn't do anything wrong. Rescue us!* But those are reactionary prayers.

Paul's prayers were quite different. We know they were different because they were prayers of worship. Prayers of worship focus on the goodness of God, not the circumstances of man. In addition to praying, they sang hymns to God. How could Paul have been worshiping God after all that? Because his relationship with God was deep. Paul would continue to pray because he was more focused on his relationship with God than a transaction. Because of that, Paul was given another event—and if he hadn't been in tune with God, he would have missed its purpose.

> Suddenly there was such a violent earthquake that the foundations of the prison were shaken. At once all the prison doors flew open, and everyone's chains came loose. (Acts 16:26)

If you were in that situation, what else could you possibly pray for besides the doors opening and your chains falling off? This was poetic justice at its finest. If I were in Paul's position, that's exactly what I would have been praying for. As soon as the doors opened and the chains fell off, I would have started running for the door without looking back.

However, Paul saw this from a different perspective. Because he had been communicating with God before his imprisonment, he knew that God desired something different from him. Paul realized that this event was bigger than he was. It wasn't just about his wrongful accusation or being thrown in jail. God was at work, and the fulfillment of his plan would take the healing of a demon-possessed girl, the wrongful accusation of a crowd, flogging and unmerciful beatings, a prison sentence, and finally a perfect opportunity to escape. Paul recognized all that and did something astonishing.

> The jailer woke up, and when he saw the prison doors open, he drew his sword and was about to kill himself because

he thought the prisoners had escaped. But Paul shouted, "Don't harm yourself! We are all here!" (Acts 16:27–28)

What? *"We are all here?"* Are you kidding me? With everything that had happened, Paul didn't bolt for the door. There's nothing logical about that decision. But Paul was being proactive and not reactive. A reactive prayer to the unfair beating and jailing would have been to ask for a way out. When the earthquake came, certainly that could have been classified as the way out. But the proactive prayer was, *God, you are in control, and if you want me to stay here, I will. Just tell me what to do.*

The jailer called for lights, rushed in and fell trembling before Paul and Silas. He then brought them out and asked, "Sirs, what must I do to be saved?"

They replied, "Believe in the Lord Jesus, and you will be saved—you and your household." Then they spoke the word of the Lord to him and to all the others in his house. At that hour of the night the jailer took them and washed their wounds; then immediately he and all his household were baptized. The jailer brought them into his house and set a meal before them; he was filled with joy because he had come to believe in God—he and his whole household. (Acts 16:29–34)

If Paul had prayed specifically for an answer to this particular situation, he might have fled the jail as soon as he had the opportunity. Consider the chain of events that ultimately led to the salvation of the jailer and his family. If Paul hadn't been wrongfully accused, he wouldn't have been in jail. If Paul hadn't healed the slave girl, he wouldn't have been wrongfully accused. If he had not spent time in prayer, he wouldn't have healed the girl. And if none of those events had occurred, the jailer and his entire household would have missed the opportunity not only to hear the gospel but to see it witnessed in the life of Paul, then to believe and be baptized.

The events in our lives are never just about the events. When we initiate prayer at the time when God calls us to action, rarely will we act in boldness and faith. While we ask for God's guidance and favor, he knows there is more at stake than our current circumstances.

THE RELIGIOUS CYCLE VERSUS THE DISCIPLESHIP CYCLE

How we pray has a dramatic effect on our internal and external lives, and it greatly affects the way we are able to become disciples of Jesus. The rest of this book will be spent looking at two distinct cycles we can take with our prayer lives. Those who only pray and fail to act live in what I call the Religious Cycle. Those who stop praying and start doing live in what I call the Discipleship Cycle.

Both cycles are dangerous, but for different reasons. The Religious Cycle is dangerous because what it promises is unobtainable. It will leave you empty and disappointed. The Discipleship Cycle is dangerous because it requires action that may be risky, and it demands a greater level of faith. It will cause others to think you are crazy, but the level of peace it brings is unmatched. Getting into the Religious Cycle is easy, but leaving is extremely difficult. If you can leave the Religious Cycle, joining the Discipleship Cycle is possible. If you can stay in the Discipleship Cycle, your life will include a level of peace, faith, and excitement you never imagined possible.

But the Discipleship Cycle is not for the faint of heart. This cycle caused Peter to leave his family business and ultimately die for his faith. It caused Nehemiah to risk his life numerous times just to endure hard manual labor. It caused Elisabeth Elliot to return to the tribe that murdered her husband (more on this later). The Discipleship Cycle will demand your life. When Jesus taught the crowds what it meant to be his disciple, he told them to estimate the cost—to consider if it would be worth it. This is the cost of the Discipleship Cycle:

> Whoever wants to be my disciple must deny themselves and take up their cross daily and follow me. For whoever wants to save their life will lose it, but whoever loses their life for me will save it. (Luke 9:23–24)

The Religious Cycle is made up of three main components: procrastination, isolation, and pride. All three of these components work in opposition to taking up your cross daily. They deceive you into thinking prayer is the only thing that matters to God. In the next chapters, we will explore the components of the Religious Cycle to see if you are falling victim to them.

CHAPTER 4

PRAYER AS PROCRASTINATION

PUTTING OFF UNTIL TOMORROW WHAT WE SHOULD DO TODAY seems to be inherent to our sinful nature. Whether it's cleaning out the garage, paying the bills, or starting a diet, we know we should start today; but for some reason we continue to put it off until the next day, and the next, and the next. Once we fall into this pattern, it continues day after day, week after week, year after year. It wouldn't be so bad if we could contain this behavior to just our exercise or diets. But procrastination shows up uninvited in all the other areas of our lives. Before we know it, it has made its way into our prayer lives.

What a tragedy it is to wake up ten years later, still praying about obeying God's call from a decade ago. But this happens more often than you might think. God calls, and instead of acting, we pray. And we continue to pray until we can't even remember when he originally called us.

It's easy to justify using prayer as procrastination; the goal really is to do what God has called us to do—just tomorrow.

Yes, we will apologize—but we'll do it tomorrow. Yes, we will tithe—but we'll do it tomorrow (when we have enough money). Yes, we will take that new job across the globe—but we'll do it tomorrow (when a raise is certain).

Yes—but always tomorrow. Saying yes for tomorrow makes us feel spiritually safe. We justify our obedience because we technically haven't said no to God. It's not as if we're running, like Jonah did when he was called to preach to the wicked people in Nineveh (Jonah 1). *We will go to Nineveh, God, but we'll do it tomorrow.* We haven't refused God—technically. But obedience by technicality is missing the point entirely.

If we are honest, we don't want God to use technicalities with us. Do we want prayers answered technically? When we're praying for a new job, do we really want just any job? When we're praying for a spouse, do we really want the first person who says hello? When we're praying for those who truly matter to us, do we really want a technical blessing? The answer to all these questions is no. Of course we don't. We pray knowing that he knows us inside out, that he is intimately acquainted with our souls, and that he will act in the way that is best for us—not just giving an answer that covers the bare minimum like a genie might. So why do we try to convince ourselves that we're acting according to God's will when we say, "Yes, but tomorrow"?

One of the reasons we procrastinate is that we don't trust God. If we believed that his decision really was best for us, we would act on it today, not wanting to wait one more day. If we're honest with ourselves, we don't think that repairing that broken relationship will be worth it. We don't believe it's best to raise our kids in that country. We truly don't trust that starting a church will matter. We want to say yes so we can remain obedient; so we choose to continue to pray about it instead of acting. But when we do that, we are misusing prayer as procrastination.

DON'T LET "I DON'T KNOW HOW" STOP YOU

When I was younger, I wanted to play guitar. I would see others play and wish it was me. There was a big problem, though: I didn't know how to play the guitar. I wanted to, but I didn't know how. Then, one day, a light bulb lit up. It seemed that all the bands I loved and the guitarists I admired also didn't know how to play the guitar at some point. No one came from the womb playing guitar. They all had to learn from scratch. That was such a freeing thought. At some point in time, they all wanted to play guitar but didn't know how.

Think about it. There was a time when the Wright brothers couldn't fly a plane. There was a time when Abraham Lincoln had no idea how to be president. There was a time when Leonardo da Vinci had yet to use a paintbrush. There was a time when William Shakespeare had no clue how to write. There was a time when Steve Jobs didn't know what a computer was.

The same is true for whatever it is God is calling you to do. If you don't know how to do it, that's okay. Neither did others who answered the call. Not knowing is actually a rite of passage to accomplishing something big. So how does one go from not knowing to knowing? It's simple: by doing.

I eventually learned how to play guitar by buying a guitar and practicing it every day. Praying about it didn't help. Looking at the guitar didn't help. Watching TV didn't help. Buying guitar picks and strings didn't help. It was only when I picked up the guitar and started strumming and plucking strings that I started to learn.

The Wright brothers actually had to *build* a plane before they learned how to fly. Andy Stanley had to stand in front of people and teach. Donald Miller had to sit in front of his computer and start typing. Not knowing how to do what God has called you to do isn't a valid excuse. We all have to learn, and the best way to learn is to do. You can pray all you want for God to show you how to do something, but if you really want to learn, it's time for you to take a jump.

WE'RE WAITING FOR YOU TO JUMP

Our obedience can have a broader effect than we realize. It can directly impact others in our lives. If we don't act on what God has called us to do, others may not be able to act on what God is calling them to do either. Sometimes we have to go first.

I recently had the opportunity to sit down with Perry Noble, pastor of NewSpring Church in Anderson, South Carolina. What follows is part of the story of how God took a small Bible study on a college campus and transformed it into a church of more than twenty thousand people. One of the things that makes this story so compelling is where it takes place. Anderson, South Carolina, is not a bustling metropolis.

There are only about twenty-six thousand people inside the city limits. At the time I spoke with Perry, the closest Starbucks was thirty minutes away! I'll let Perry share the story in his own words:

Thirteen years ago, I was sitting in front of the TV on a Saturday night watching the Weather Channel, begging God to stop the ice storm I saw headed toward my town. Years of planning, prayer, and preparation had culminated in the launching of our new church the previous Sunday. Now it looked as if there would be no week two. I prayed my guts out that night and went to bed anxious to see a miracle the next morning.

When I woke up on Sunday, not only did the storm hit, but it hit worse than anyone expected. The power was out all across the city, including the college building in which we were to hold the service. Trees were down. The roads were covered in ice. It was obvious we weren't supposed to have church that day.

Since our church was all of one week old, we had no way of communicating with our attendees. I lived close enough to walk to the building, so I bundled up and headed out. I made a little note that said "Church Canceled Today."

I came around the corner of the building, heading toward the main entrance. I grabbed the note and was reaching to attach it to the door when I heard, "Hey! We're still having church today, right? You're not canceling because of the weather, are you?"

I turned around and there was a young couple who had

driven into town, braving the roads to come to church. My heart was pounding. I didn't think anyone would come, but if they were brave enough to be here, then perhaps others would too.

"No way!" I yelled back.

I quickly crumpled the sign in my hand and stashed it in my pocket. Little did they know how close I had been to posting that sign. We went inside the building and began to set up chairs, not knowing if anyone would show up. It was freezing cold with no heat; were it not for a few windows, it would have been completely dark. We sat down for a few moments, and I prayed for people to show up.

A few minutes later, some college kids started dropping in. By the time the service started, seventy people had shown up. We sang some songs, I preached, and we even brought in a four-hundred-dollar offering. I guess God really knew what he was doing.

It all started years earlier when God spoke through two different seminary professors. First, I was in a systematic theology class when the professor brought up church planting. This was a relatively new concept to me. I'd read Rick Warren's *Purpose Driven Church*, but other than that, I was unfamiliar with the details.

I raised my hand to ask the professor, who is now the president of a major seminary, a question.

"I think planting churches may be a dumb idea," I said. "Why in the world would you start something new when there are so many existing churches that could be improved?"

He looked at me patiently and replied, "It's easier to give birth to a baby than to resurrect the dead."

I wrote down that line in my notes. Looking back, it was one of the most influential statements on my life. That same semester, the professor of my apologetics class opened one of his lectures by saying, "I'm going to show you the most effective way to evangelize the world."

Because I'm an evangelist, he had my attention immediately. I want to see people come to know Jesus. I was expecting some new theory or technique, but it wasn't either of those.

"The single best way to evangelize the world is through church planting," he announced.

After that statement, I surrendered my life to this calling. I knew I was going to start a church; I just didn't know how or when.

After seminary, I was serving as a youth pastor at a local church while living and working part-time on a college campus. I started a Bible study at the college, and in six weeks we went from eight people to one hundred fifty. The call to plant a church was still there, but I didn't think it would happen until much further in the future. It would take a step of faith before the door opened.

The on-campus Bible study was gaining a lot of traction. I spoke with a good friend one night in the parking lot. I was still trying to figure out what God was doing, and in turn what I was supposed to do. The idea of planting a church had been thrown around, but I wasn't sure. I wasn't fully committed to the movement that was building.

I said to him, "It's like we're all standing on the edge of a cliff, just waiting for something to happen." I was just haphazardly throwing the analogy out there, not expecting a response.

"We *are* waiting on something to happen," he replied. "We're waiting for you to jump. Because as soon as you jump, we'll all follow. But you've got to jump first."

That was the final straw. I decided to jump, which meant I needed to resign from the church where I was working. I was sure that if I took that step, God would show me what to do next.

The very day after I decided to resign, I had lunch with a good friend who asked me what I would attempt for God if I knew I couldn't fail. We were sitting in Red Lobster, enjoying the delicious Cheddar Bay biscuits. Little did I know that my future was about to drastically change. I knew immediately what I would do.

"I'd start a church," I replied.

He quickly responded, "Well, you're a coward if you don't."

From there, things started moving very rapidly; I knew it was time to go for it. Five months later, I prayed for God to stop an ice storm and allow us to meet for the second time as a new church. God didn't stop the ice storm, but he allowed us to have church that day, and little did I know how many thousands of people would be affected because I decided to jump.

That was thirteen years ago. In the subsequent years, God has done more than I ever imagined in the small city of

Anderson, South Carolina. We've grown from a small Bible study of eight people into a church of more than twenty-five thousand attendees at eight campuses across the state. Halfway through 2013, we've seen more than five thousand people place their faith in Christ.

Sometimes you have to jump first. What if your jump is the catalyst for others to do what God is calling them to do? Then would you do it? If you were willing to seek reconciliation for a broken relationship, maybe doing so would allow the other person to not only heal your relationship but repair others in his or her life as well. If you were willing to write that book, maybe it could touch hundreds or even thousands of people in ways you couldn't even imagine. If you were willing to start that business, think of how many people could benefit—especially the people who aren't called to start a business but are called to work for one like yours.

Jumping first isn't easy. It's scary. There are dozens of excuses for not jumping. But you need to realize that your jump may be the event that others are waiting for to make *their* jumps.

What would have happened if Perry only prayed about starting a church and never jumped into action? How many people would have missed hearing the gospel? How many staff members would have stayed in their other jobs and never gotten to work at the church? When Perry jumped, he gave others permission to jump, and as a result tens of thousands of lives have been impacted by the cumulative work of those who followed.

Is it time for you to jump?

CHAPTER 5

PRAYER AS ISOLATION

A DOMINANT THEME THROUGHOUT THE NARRATIVE OF Scripture, from creation all the way to the modern church, is the importance of community. Before creation, we see the beauty of community in the relationships between the Father, Son, and Holy Spirit. After God created Adam, he said that it was not good for man to be alone, so he created Eve to be Adam's partner. When the Israelites became a nation, God gave them the law, mainly so they would know how to live and prosper in community. The ministry of Jesus was done primarily in the context of community—sometimes with twelve disciples, other times with only three. The early church was founded through the work of community. Through sharing and serving, the early church prospered, even during times of turmoil and persecution. Community is essential for living the life God has called you to live.

When we use prayer as isolation, we violate the principles of community. We don't allow others to truly connect with us, which makes it impossible for them to know how to pray for and serve us. Community is impossible when relationships remain at a surface level. Sometimes, without knowing it, our prayers isolate us from the godly council and encouragement we most desperately need.

How do we use prayer as isolation? Practically, it looks like the following scenario. Let's say that I feel God has called me to talk with my neighbor about the gospel. During church small group, I ask that everyone pray with me for the right time to share with him. This is a good thing. From an outside perspective, everyone sees that I love my neighbor because I want to share with him. Everyone gets to see how I am praying for my neighbor. I am spiritual. I am loving. Or at least that's what they'll think. But what happens the next week when someone brings it up, and I respond with, "I'm still praying"? Not much. They still think I'm spiritual. They still think I'm loving. No one thinks to call me out on the fact that God has called me to something that I'm not following through on.

What happens if this goes on for weeks, and then months? By avoiding having to share with my neighbor, even though I may be praying about it, at some point I become disobedient. Even more, I hide behind prayer and isolate myself from my community by keeping them from knowing what really lies in my heart.

Using prayer as isolation is rooted in pride and fear, all while being expressed as individualism. In the above example, the reality is that I don't want to tell you how afraid I am to share with my neighbor. My pride doesn't want you to know what's really happening in my heart. When I tell you that I'm still praying about it, I'm isolating myself from further inquiries, putting up a thicker wall between my heart and the community, and hoping you assume everything is fine. The isolated heart says, "I can do this on my own and don't need your help." This is the trap of the Religious Cycle. You procrastinate, and because of pride you isolate. When someone presses you on your progress, you isolate yourself, and in turn you procrastinate even more. The cycle keeps spinning.

A ROOM WITH A VIEW

As the process of isolation grows, it begins to affect other areas of our lives. We eventually move toward justifying other acts that we wouldn't be proud to share. This isn't something that just happens to spiritual newborns. It happens to experienced, godly men and women.

In the Old Testament, we're told that King David was a man after God's own heart. In other words, David was a man who knew the heart of God and had a very intimate relationship with him. But David began to isolate himself from community and hid his thoughts. Instead of doing what was expected of him as king, he had a critical lapse in judgment.

In 2 Samuel, we learn that kings usually went off to war in the spring, but David chose not to do this. Instead, he sent his army with another leader so that he could remain behind. The isolation had already begun. Instead of doing what God had called him to do, he pushed the responsibility onto others.

Since David wasn't fighting, he had a lot of free time on his hands and decided one evening to look out from the penthouse on the surrounding neighbors.

One evening David got up from his bed and walked around on the roof of the palace. From the roof he saw a woman bathing. The woman was very beautiful, and David sent someone to find out about her. (2 Sam. 11:2–3)

Many aspects of this story baffle me. In a moment of weakness, David saw Bathsheba, a beautiful woman, naked from a distance. I'm not sure why Bathsheba was bathing where David could see her. Maybe she wasn't in the wide open and he had to do some maneuvering to see her. If she couldn't see him, does that mean David was peeking through the wall so he wouldn't be seen? These are all warning signs.

The story continues its oddness when David seeks help in identifying the naked woman. This begs more questions. Would you feel awkward asking another guy to help you identify a naked woman in a bathtub on the roof of a nearby house?

The man David sent reported back and said, "She is Bathsheba, the daughter of Eliam and the wife of Uriah the Hittite" (2 Sam. 11:3).

So apparently the man knew who the beautiful naked woman was. This makes you wonder if he had seen her bathing too. Or maybe they were grade-school friends. Regardless, he knew who she was and that she was married.

David continued to miss the warning signs, and the story

takes a drastic turn in the wrong direction: "Then David sent messengers to get her" (2 Sam. 11:4).

Evidently, the man decided not to speak out to the king directly. We don't know if he tried to drive home to David the fact that this woman was married by using a tone or a look. Maybe his reply was more like, "Isn't this . . . Bath . . . she . . . ba? The *wife* . . . of Ur . . . i . . . ah?" In other words, maybe he tried. We don't know, but off the men went to get her. The Hebrew word used here literally means "to take her"—which shows that David had already made up his mind about what he was going to do.[1]

David did not stop there. The next line leaves no room for mistake: "She came to him, and he slept with her" (2 Sam. 11:4).

After lusting after her in his heart, he continued in his sin and committed adultery. The narrator lets us know that she had purified herself from her uncleanness (meaning her monthly cycle), which meant she definitely wasn't pregnant before her evening detour at the palace. Sometime after returning home, however, Bathsheba realized she was pregnant and sent word to David.

From here, the story gets even worse. After neglecting his leadership role, David fell into lust, which grew to adultery, which turned to deceit, and ultimately ended in murder. Hollywood couldn't make up a movie with this much drama.

> In the morning David wrote a letter to Joab and sent it with Uriah. In it he wrote, "Put Uriah out in front where the fighting is fiercest. Then withdraw from him so he will be struck down and die." (2 Sam. 11:14–15)

To cover up the sin in his heart, David continued down the path of terrible decision making, ending in murder.

> When Uriah's wife heard that her husband was dead, she mourned for him. After the time of mourning was over, David had her brought to his house, and she became his wife and bore him a son. (2 Sam. 11:26–27)

To make matters even worse, the chapter ends on an ominous note: "But the thing David had done displeased the LORD" (2 Sam. 11:27).

This sad story in the otherwise amazing life of David brings up a few important lessons we should consider. One, no one is above temptation. If a man after God's own heart can fall into such sin, don't assume it can't happen to you. That type of thinking is prideful and dangerous.

Two, David faced temptation because he wasn't obedient to what God had called him to do. Part of his job and calling as the king was to lead his army into battle. It wasn't as if this was a surprise for him, since he had previously led the army to battle many times. Instead, for reasons we do not know, he passed on his responsibility and stayed home. He shouldn't have even been home on the roof to see Bathsheba.

Three, when we isolate ourselves from community, we are much more likely to make poor decisions. Keep communication open with those in your life. Don't simply tell people that you're praying about something to stop an inquiry. Allow them to push you toward action.

LOVE YOUR NEIGHBOR

On multiple occasions, Jesus mentioned that loving your neighbor as yourself sums up the entire law and is what God desires for us (Matt. 22:38–40). Using prayer as isolation makes loving your neighbor very difficult. When you aren't open, you cannot engage—and it takes engagement to love your neighbors.

There's a great scene in Luke where an expert in the law tried to justify his lack of engaging his neighbors to Jesus.

On one occasion an expert in the law stood up to test Jesus. "Teacher," he asked, "what must I do to inherit eternal life?"

"What is written in the Law?" [Jesus] replied. "How do you read it?"

He answered: "'Love the Lord your God with all your heart and with all your soul and with all your strength and with all your mind'; and, 'Love your neighbor as yourself.'"

"You have answered correctly," Jesus replied. "Do this and you will live."

But he wanted to justify himself, so he asked Jesus, "And who is my neighbor?" (Luke 10:25–29)

Instead of bluntly calling him out, Jesus shared this story:

"A man was going down from Jerusalem to Jericho, when he was attacked by robbers. They stripped him of his clothes, beat him and went away, leaving him half dead. A priest happened to be going down the same road, and when he saw the man, he passed by on the other side. So too, a Levite, when he came to the place and saw him, passed by on the other side. But a Samaritan, as he traveled, came where the man was; and when he saw him, he took pity on him. He went to him and bandaged his wounds, pouring on oil and wine. Then he put the man on his own donkey, brought him to an inn and took care of him. The next day he took out two denarii and gave them to the innkeeper. 'Look after him,' he said, 'and when I return, I will reimburse you for any extra expense you may have.'

"Which of these three do you think was a neighbor to the man who fell into the hands of robbers?"

The expert in the law replied, "The one who had mercy on him."

Jesus told him, "Go and do likewise." (Luke 10:30–37)

Most likely you've heard this story multiple times. Dubbed the parable of the good Samaritan, this story is useful to pastors who want to make various points in their teaching about how we are to love our neighbors. Some will use this to show that anyone can make a difference, even if you're an outcast of society, as the Samaritan was in this story. Others will show that even the religious fall short of what's expected of them, as the Levite and the priest did.

However, I want to look at another angle. Throughout Scripture, we are called to love our neighbors. This command started back in Genesis, made its way through the law and prophets, and eventually led to the teachings of Jesus and the apostles.

In Matthew 5, Jesus said,

You have heard that it was said, "Love your neighbor and hate your enemy." But I tell you, love your enemies and pray for those who persecute you, that you may be children of your Father in heaven. He causes his sun to rise on the evil and the good, and sends rain on the righteous and the unrighteous. If you love those who love you, what reward will you get? Are not even the tax collectors doing that? And if you greet only your own people, what are you doing more than others? Do not even pagans do that? Be perfect, therefore, as your heavenly Father is perfect. (vv. 5:43–48)

The interesting thing about the good Samaritan parable is that prayer isn't mentioned once. Jesus doesn't tell the expert in the law to pray. In the parable, the Levite and the priest not only fail to stop and help the man, but neither of them prays for him either. Then again, neither does the Samaritan! Jesus is illustrating what it looks like to love our neighbors as ourselves, and prayer isn't even mentioned. I find that interesting.

So what is mentioned? The Samaritan did what every single one of us would have wanted if we had just been beaten and left for dead. We would want someone to help us out of the ditch and get us medical attention. At a bare minimum, we'd want someone to call the police and take us to the hospital. What the beaten man isn't screaming for is prayer. While praying for him would most definitely show him love, he was going to die if he didn't get help, and prayer alone would have been pointless. The man needed medical help, food, and a chance to recover—exactly what the Samaritan delivered.

Two important ideas are presented here. One, loving our neighbors isn't something we have to pray about doing. When asked how to sum up the entire Old Testament law, Jesus said to love the Lord your God with all your heart, soul, mind, and strength, and to love your neighbor as yourself (Luke 10:27). Jesus said that people would recognize his disciples because they loved one another (John 13:35). Loving our neighbors is a given. If you come to a decision where one option would be to love your neighbor and the other would be to not love your neighbor, then rest comfortably; there's no need to pray about it. No need to ask God which way you should go. You are to love your neighbor every time. Did you notice in the story that the priest and the Levite were criticized because they didn't help, not because they didn't pray? This isn't meant to discredit the value of prayer, but rather to assign the proper value to action.

NOT-SO-QUIET AFTERNOON

A few years ago, my wife, Betsey, and I were enjoying a laid-back Saturday afternoon. The winter Olympics were on, and I was finally getting to watch some skiing. (I'd missed most of it because I'd been working late most of the week.) I was just settling in when I heard a knock at the door. My wife looked at me and I said, "I'm not getting it. It's probably just the neighbor kids playing games like they always do."

My wife is a teacher and knows all the neighborhood

children. We are frequent victims of the knock-and-run. She looked at me, insisting I answer it.

"I'm not getting it." I held my ground.

"Fine," she said. "I'll get it."

She got off the couch and headed for the door. Before she was able to unlock the door, someone banged on it again.

"Coming!" she replied.

When she opened the door, Bridgette, our neighbor, was yelling and flustered. "Your house is on fire! Get out here, quickly. Hurry!"

"What?!"

I jumped off the couch, bolted out the garage without shoes, and rounded the side of the house. All the dormant Bermuda grass between my neighbor's house and ours was burning. The pine straw next to my house was beginning to burn, as was the vinyl siding. Our neighbor's house was starting to catch too. The siding burned very quickly, and in a matter of minutes the fire was already a few feet off the ground. At that rate, in another few minutes, the flames would hit the roof and the whole house would catch fire.

Now, let me pause right here and tell you what I didn't want my neighbors to do. I didn't want them to come to the door and say, "Just wanted to let you know your house is on fire, but don't worry, our whole family is praying for you. Praying for rain, my friend, praying for rain."

At that moment, I didn't want to hear prayers that the fire would go out. I didn't want to hear prayers that it would suddenly start snowing. In the heat of the moment (pun very much intended), I didn't want any prayer. I wanted all hands on deck trying to put out the fire before my house turned into the neighborhood barbecue pit.

I ran to the back of my house, trying to find our hose. Bridgette's husband, Oscar, was pulling his hose toward the fire as I came running to the back of the house.

"Find the fire extinguisher!" I yelled to Betsey. She took off to look in the garage.

I dragged our hose around the back of the house and started spraying the siding with as much water as I could.

Betsey came around the front and yelled, "I can't find it!"

"Then keep looking. And call 911!"

I was starting to make a little difference on my side of the fire. I had put out the fire halfway up the side of the house. The vinyl siding was burning quickly in the middle, though. I sprayed the house, then turned my attention back to the pine straw so that it wouldn't spread any farther. I continued spraying the water, but it seemed to be coming out so slowly. Only half the fire was out on our house, and I hadn't even touched my neighbor's house yet.

I noticed the fire was spreading toward my neighbor's natural gas line. We had to put it out soon to avoid the risk of an explosion. As I continued to spray, Oscar came running around the house with two fire extinguishers. He sprayed the first one on the front side of my house, which now was only about twelve feet away from me.

I was getting close to putting out all the fire on my side, so I pointed toward his house. "No, Oscar! Spray around the gas line!"

He was only able to spray for about twenty seconds, since the extinguishers were those little kitchen ones. Just then, Betsey came running around back with our extinguisher. It was a large one, and she passed it off to Oscar. He grabbed it, started spraying his house, and completely put the fire out. He then ran to my house and sprayed what was left.

In a few minutes, we had put out both fires, limiting the damage and avoiding an explosion. I continued to spray around the house and on the siding just in case there were any sparks left over that we couldn't see.

The smell of burnt plastic floated through the smoky air as I surveyed the damage. The fire had gotten about one-third of the way up the side of my house and a little higher up my neighbor's. Thankfully, no one was hurt, and the damage was minimal compared to what it could have been. All this happened in less than twenty minutes.

I continued to wet the ground around the burn site as we heard sirens, and the fire trucks started showing up. The volunteer fire response team jumped off the trucks and began pulling their hoses to find that the three of us had put it out with a garden hose, two kitchen extinguishers, and one large extinguisher. Needless to say, I wasn't too pleased with their response time, but was thankful that both my neighbor and I had been home to put out the fire.

Would it have been loving if my neighbor had just prayed about the fire instead of warning us? How about if they'd knocked and told us about the fire and decided to kneel down while I was running around with hoses and fire extinguishers trying to put it out? Would it have been loving if I had put out the fire on my house and just prayed about my neighbor's house as it burned?

The obvious answers are no, no, and no. There are times when praying for your neighbor isn't really loving them at all. There are times when action is the only expression of love. In these times, you don't have to pray about whether God wants you to love your neighbor. He's already told us to. The question is, will you?

CHAPTER 6

PRAYER AS PRIDE

IF YOU WALK WITH GOD LONG ENOUGH, SOMEDAY YOU'LL respond to his prompting like this: "You want me to do what?!" Out of nowhere, he'll want you to move across the country, or even to the other side of the world. He'll want you to sell your business or start a new one. He may call you back to your hometown to minister to those who drove you away years ago. Or maybe he wants you to start a ministry to reach the porn industry, which is what happened to my friend Mike.

Even when you pray and feel confident in God's calling, the fear of what others will think becomes a reality when you reach the point of no return. This concern often grows deeper and becomes a disease that is the last component of the Religious Cycle.

No person is immune from this disease. It can strike the rich and poor, men and women, children and adults. It knows no boundaries of race or geography. No scientific advancement has ever been able to rid the world of this deadly disease. Those who have it rarely realize it. We are all carriers. This disease is known as pride.

Pride is having an image of one's self that is far higher than it should be and an image of others that is far lower. Pride ignores the problems in one's self and highlights them in others. Pride is unforgiving of everyone, except of the proud person. Pride causes us to reveal only parts of who we are, fearful of what will happen if others know the full story. If we aren't careful, pride will stop us from being obedient when God calls us.

The following is my friend Mike's story of God telling him to walk through that door.

I was standing on the loading deck at the back entrance to the convention center connected to the Venetian Hotel in Las Vegas, Nevada. The other people with me were unloading the Suburban, but I kept staring at the hotel door. I knew that as soon as I walked through that door, there was no turning back. That door represented the point of no return.

All the conversations up until then had led us to that door. One side of the door was safe. There were no strange looks. No whispers behind my back. I could walk away and no one would notice. But the other side of the door was the world of the unknown. In there was fear. What would people think? What would they say? My heart was beating a hundred miles an hour. Crossing over the threshold of that door would change everything.

I remember when I decided to tell my parents what I

was going to do. There's really no good way to say, "Mom, Dad, I'm going to start ministering at porn shows." Those words were hard to get out.

We were at a family barbecue on a beautiful California afternoon. The smell of burgers and hot dogs wafted off the grill. Knowing there was no easy way, I just decided to tell them: "In January, we're officially launching XXX Church in Las Vegas, at a porn convention, to minister to people with porn struggles."

Gulp. The silence lasted only a few seconds, but it seemed like years. I went on to explain what we were doing and why. I described the vision for the ministry and the impact it could make.

After getting out my spiel, their responses were honestly about as good as I could have hoped for. They were supportive more of me than the idea. I don't think they totally got it, but that's to be expected with most burdens. Most people never fully appreciate your idea the way you do.

For the past few months, I had been praying about this very moment. Ever since a fateful conversation with a friend at P.F. Chang's, I had known that this day would come.

I was working at a church as the communications director, but also volunteering with the student ministry on Wednesdays. In my work with the students, the issue of porn kept creeping up. The problem was, there didn't seem to be anyone willing to really talk about the issue from all sides. We needed to be able to discuss the issues of grace, guilt, forgiveness, confession, and healing in a safe environment. Everything seemed so focused on hate and condemnation that I was convinced there needed to be another voice in the conversation. This was the beginning of XXX Church.

Our first step was to create a website to share some resources and provide a safe place for discussion. I partnered with a friend who was already doing student ministry, and from there we were off and running. We knew that just praying about this wouldn't make the impact we wanted. It was obvious that we needed to get more involved, and that meant paying five thousand dollars for a booth, driving to Vegas, and walking through the door.

So there I was in Las Vegas, with my wife and a few friends, about to launch a ministry at the world's largest porn convention. And as soon as I walked through that door, there was no turning back. Walking through the door meant dealing with very real fears. I was worried about how people would respond when they found out we were Christians. Would they get violent? Would they kick us out? Would this be an utter failure?

Serious fears were swelling in my brain. But I knew why we had come. So we walked in, found our spot, and set up our booth. We had brought a professional trade-show backdrop that said "XXXChurch.com: The Number 1 Christian Porn Site." We had matching T-shirts and some small handout cards. While we were setting up, we met the people at the booths on either side of us. On the right side was a porn animation company. I had no idea there was even a market for that.

We spent the next few days talking with anyone who came by our booth. We handed out some cards and had some good conversations. This would be the first of many visits to porn conventions. At future visits we would hand out Bibles that said "Jesus Loves Porn Stars."

Our whole desire was to let people know that there was someone there who loved them and cared about them, no matter what their struggles.

"You can't go *there*. Seriously. There are many places you can go, but that's not one of them. What will people think? You know they'll talk. Think of the potential danger. What about your marriage? Your family? How could you possibly explain this to your wife? The risks are too high."

I wonder how many times Mike tried to talk himself out of what God was calling him to do. If it had been me, it would have been dozens of times. Every day. What makes the situation even more interesting is how easy it would have been to justify *not* doing what God was asking. There are even plenty of Bible verses Mike could have used in his case against what God called him to do. When you have a verse up your sleeve, it's easy to ignore when God calls you. Certainly God would not be calling a married Christian man in his thirties to go to porn conventions and mingle with *those* people. There are some things God never wants his people to see, right?

When you misuse prayer because of pride, your inaction is rooted in the fear of what others think of you. You might be so afraid to follow through with what God has called you to do that instead of doing it, you simply pray about it. Pride won't allow us to admit that we care what others think of us. Moving across the country is scary. Selling a business takes guts. Ministering at a porn convention is just crazy. But Mike's story is relevant because he was fearful of being obedient too. He had plenty of reasons to be fearful. It would have been very easy for Mike to just tell his friends he was praying about starting XXX Church. Most people would have been wowed that he was praying about it, even without him actually acting on the prayer.

A PROMISE

We may not be able to ever fully get over our fear when God calls us to something that scares us. Whether we go to minister at porn conventions or move to Egypt, fear will most likely go with us. But when we humble ourselves and admit our fear, God's hand lifts us up and strengthens us in our time of need. For those he calls, he never leaves. Listen to this promise:

I took you from the ends of the earth,
from its farthest corners I called you.
I said, 'You are my servant';
I have chosen you and have not rejected you.
So do not fear, for I am with you;
do not be dismayed, for I am your God.
I will strengthen you and help you;
I will uphold you with my righteous right hand. (Isa. 41:9–10)

Don't let fear stop you from doing what God has called you to do. Use prayer as a time to admit your fear. Then, with

God's strength, stop praying and start doing. Saying yes can be downright scary, but God promises he will be with you. If the Maker of the universe is with you, what more do you really need? It's important to truly grasp this before you face the fearful situation of saying yes, and it's not as easy as it sounds.

Looking back, saying one particular yes was one of the scariest of my life; it was also one of the best. It all started one night when my wife, Betsey, and I were getting ready for bed. I was sitting up reading a book, as I usually do before trying to fall asleep. She climbed into bed, leaned over, and put her head on my shoulder.

"I've got an idea, but you're going to think I'm crazy," she said. "So please let me get it all out before you say anything."

I placed the book facedown on my lap. "Okay."

"I've been thinking and praying a lot lately about this, and I think we should become foster parents."

This was not at all what I was expecting. Thoughts started flying through my head of all the reasons we should *not* become foster parents. My ministry was still only a few years old and not financially viable yet. I was also going to seminary full time, and trying to graduate before we had children.

My plan was to have two biological children, then potentially adopt a third. But two years into the plan, it wasn't working out that way. I sat there for a few minutes in silence. Finally I spoke.

"There's no way. How in the world could we possibly do that right now? You're working full time. I'm working full time and going to school. Who would watch the baby? How in the world could we cope with taking care of a baby for a few weeks and then losing him or her when social services comes to take him or her away?"

I think it actually sounded harsher when I said it. Looking back, I realize what was coming out was fear rooted in pride. I had no idea how to take care of a baby. What would people think when they heard I was going to be a father? I had no idea how we could afford a baby, since adopting is typically very expensive. And what would people think about the decision to adopt now, knowing I was in the middle of running a start-up ministry? As much as you might think you're ready for a baby, I realized you never really are.

Betsey didn't say much, but I could tell she was upset. And rightly so. I had done exactly what she had told me not to do— I'd shot down her idea before it left the ground. It was difficult for me to fall asleep that night—partly because I knew I'd been a horrible husband and partly because I was thinking about becoming a foster parent. I just didn't see how it could work.

The next morning at breakfast, I could tell Betsey was still upset. She sat down next to me and said with her sad face, "You didn't even give my idea any thought before you said no. I can't help it if I feel God has put this on my heart. I don't know why, but he has."

"I'm sorry," I told her. "You're right. I should have given it more thought. It's just hard when I don't feel that at all. What do you want me to do?"

"There's a lady coming over this week from social services to talk with us about the foster-care system. I'd like you to be there and hear her out."

Although I was still against it, I said I would be at the meeting and listen to the spiel.

A few weeks passed after the social worker came to our house. There was a stack of forms on our counter. Betsey had filled out her half, but the other half—my half—was blank. I wasn't budging. I just didn't think this was the right move.

She was still frustrated with me, and I didn't know what else to do.

"Tell you what," I said one day. "I'll spend time in prayer specifically asking God to show me if I'm being selfish in not wanting to foster. When I get back from my conference next week, let's sit back down and discuss it again."

I was leaving for four days, and little did I know that our next conversation would change everything. On returning home the following week, I was anxious to talk with Betsey. I finally felt at peace about the situation, but I wasn't sure how she would handle it.

Staring down at the ground I said, "I've been thinking about it, and I still don't feel like fostering is what we should do." I took a deep breath. "I would rather start the adoption process. It will give us a little more time to plan and adjust."

I held my breath, not looking up to see her expression.

"Okay," she said, almost jumping off the couch. "Let's do it!"

"Seriously?"

"Absolutely! I'll get started today."

"Whoa. Easy. Let's start doing some research and figure out all that's entailed."

But at that point, it was too late. She was on a mission. Within a few days, she'd looked up all the requirements for our state and for many different countries. Our hearts were drawn to adopt from overseas, so that helped narrow down the options a bit, but there were still a lot of decisions to make.

In the end, something truly miraculous happened. After talking with a neighbor who worked for a local adoption agency, we were told of a couple they worked with who had been able to adopt an infant girl from overseas, which was exactly what we were praying for.

In our research, we had discovered that we failed to meet the requirements for every other option on the table. For some countries, we weren't old enough. For other countries, we failed to meet the ridiculously high income requirements. At the end of the day, God brought us a small Christian orphanage where we met all the requirements and also could adopt an infant girl. We have since learned how amazing this really was. We've talked to many people who have adopted from overseas, and very few were able to get an infant or know the sex of the baby.

Something even more miraculous happened once we agreed to pursue the adoption. A peace came over Betsey and me like nothing we'd ever experienced before in our marriage. I can still remember that feeling. In fact, every time I think about the adoption, I still feel it. This is the type of peace Paul was writing about in Philippians:

> Do not be anxious about anything, but in every situation, by prayer and petition, with thanksgiving, present your requests to God. And the peace of God, which transcends all understanding, will guard your hearts and your minds in Christ Jesus. (Phil. 4:6–7)

In the moment when my wife and I said yes to pursuing adoption, it was just an idea, a seemingly independent decision. But God began to give us a comforting peace that confirmed that the idea was from him. So after we said yes, we stopped praying about whether or not we should adopt. That had been answered. For the future, we did two things. First, we continued to pray, but our prayers switched to figuring out the difficult road ahead rather than making the actual decision. Next, we got to work.

Adopting a child involves many steps and is a long and tedious process. While prayer is vitally important, we've learned that the government doesn't allow prayers to replace the necessary reports and forms that must be filed to process an adoption. Forms must be filed with the state, a local adoption agency, the US Immigration Office, the Social Security Administration, the Department of Homeland Security, and the Passport Office. In addition to that paperwork, there are dozens of questions to answer, copies to be made, and checks to be sent. One of the forms required a three-hour interview and inspection of our home. That interview turned into a forty-page document, which would later have to be translated into our daughter's native language. There were financial records to collect, documents to notarize, and packages to FedEx halfway around the world.

When my wife and I felt God calling us to adopt, I had many more questions than answers. We had no clue what we were doing. We had no idea how to raise a child, much less an adopted child. But we knew after praying about it that we were called to do it.

I'm glad that after we said yes, we immediately got to work.

Looking back, if we had spent two more weeks praying about what God had called us to do, we would have missed the opportunity to adopt our daughter. Two weeks after we turned in our initial paperwork, the orphanage decided to cut off all applications for new adoptions. If we had waited just two more weeks, our application would have been declined and we would have been forced to find another option. I'm sure that it would have worked out eventually, but there's no way we would have gotten our baby girl. And to think, we could have missed out on having our daughter because I was fearful of what some people might say or think. I can't imagine any other face but hers. I'm so glad we stopped praying and started doing.

The funny thing about the fear of what others will think is we're not even positive they are actually going to say something to us. It's one thing to be fearful of sharks and refuse to get in the water because you saw a shark swim by. That's based on fact: you saw it with your own two eyes. But most of the time our fear of others' opinions is based purely on a fantasy that won't come true.

When God calls you to do something that scares you, there is always more at stake than you realize. What could be at stake in your life that depends on your obedience? Don't let what others may or may not say hold you back.

CHAPTER 7

YOU'RE NOT THE ONLY ONE

WHEN GOD CALLS YOU TO DO SOMETHING, IT WILL ALWAYS affect people besides yourself. At times, the personal risk is nothing compared to what will happen to a large number of people if you *don't* act. This truth is evident in the Old Testament story of Esther.

Esther's story rivals the best rags-to-riches stories we have today. Esther was a Jew whose ancestors were taken captive by King Nebuchadnezzar and exiled to Babylon. When she was young, both her parents died, leaving her an orphan living in an exiled country far away from her own people and culture. Esther had an older cousin, Mordecai, who was also taken captive during the exile. Mordecai raised Esther as his own daughter since there was no one left to care for her.

Before Esther enters the story, it's important to know some background. The ruler of Babylon at the time was King Xerxes, an egotistical, vain leader who loved to show his greatness and refused to be questioned. Not the guy you probably want to work for. His empire stretched across the modern Middle East, ruling 127 provinces (Est. 1:1).

To demonstrate his greatness, he decided to throw a party at the royal palace. But this was no ordinary party. It lasted for 180 days! There was eating and drinking, and more eating and more drinking. After the 180 days of celebration were over, Xerxes decided that it wasn't enough, so he threw another banquet for seven days in the enclosed gardens of his palace.

> The garden had hangings of white and blue linen, fastened with cords of white linen and purple material to silver rings on marble pillars. There were couches of gold and silver on a mosaic pavement of porphyry, marble, mother-of-pearl and other costly stones. Wine was served in goblets of gold, each one different from the other, and the royal wine was abundant, in keeping with the king's liberality. By the king's command each guest was allowed to drink with no restrictions, for the king instructed all the wine stewards to serve each man what he wished. (Est. 1:6–8)

In short, Xerxes wanted everyone to know that he was the man.

On the last day of the feast, after much drinking with his men, the king gave word that he wanted his queen, Vashti, to come before him and his royal court wearing her royal crown, for she was lovely to look at. Most scholars believe he wanted her to wear nothing but her crown—parading in front of his drunken buddies like a stripper. But Vashti had self-respect and refused to come.

Then, according to the story, "the king became furious and burned with anger" (Est. 1:12). After seeking the advice of his council, the king decided he was through with Vashti and she was never allowed in the palace again. As we will later see, she was lucky to have been allowed to leave alive.

Since he no longer had a queen, Xerxes sent word across the country in search of beautiful, young virgins who could become the next queen. The most beautiful girls of the land were then brought to the king's palace to prepare to meet the king. But this was no small task.

> Before a young woman's turn came to go in to King Xerxes, she had to complete twelve months of beauty treatments prescribed for the women, six months with oil of myrrh and six with perfumes and cosmetics. (Est. 2:12)

As it turns out, Esther was picked to stand before the king. God was working on her behalf, and she caught the king's eye.

> Now the king was attracted to Esther more than to any of the other women, and she won his favor and approval more than any of the other virgins. So he set a royal crown on her head and made her queen instead of Vashti. And the king gave a great banquet, Esther's banquet, for all his nobles and officials. He proclaimed a holiday throughout the provinces and distributed gifts with royal liberality. (Est. 2:17–18)

Through the providential work of God, Esther, an orphan and a Jew, was now the queen of Babylon.

Now the story really gets interesting. While Esther was enjoying her new role as queen, her cousin, Mordecai, remained outside the confines of the palace. One day, he overheard two of the king's officers plotting an assassination and coup. Mordecai then got word to Esther, who was able to warn the king. After investigating, Xerxes discovered the plot was real and had the two officers hanged. Esther told the king that Mordecai was the real hero, which brought Mordecai to everyone's attention.

In every good drama, there is always a villain working an angle. In this story, his name is Haman. The king honored Haman and made him his highest official. This came with certain perks, including being honored by everyone, especially those in the royal court. When Mordecai refused to bow down to Haman, the other officials reported back to Haman, whose pride could not let this go unpunished. Haman decided to destroy not only Mordecai but all the Jewish people living in the kingdom.

As if sniffing out plots were his job, Mordecai found out about this plot too, and again pleaded with Esther to use her new position of influence to stop the massacre of the Jewish people.

But this time it was different. The plot didn't directly affect the king. Esther had no leverage, and she knew that if she asked for something from the king without being summoned, she could lose her life. Mordecai begged her to go before the king to plead for her people. It wasn't just Mordecai who was in danger—it was the entire nation. A genocide was being planned, and Esther was the only person who could stop it.

She was torn. The law of the land was that anyone who

went into the king's inner court without first being summoned would be put to death. No questions. Immediately. Dead (Est. 4:11).

Well, there was one exception. If the king extended his gold scepter toward you as you approached, then you were spared, for he had literally extended you grace. Esther had most likely seen the king exercise this law on occasion.

To make matters worse, she told Mordecai that she had not been summoned before the king in thirty days. In other words, he had other women currently meeting his needs. She wasn't even on his radar—a bad thing, considering what she planned to do. But Mordecai convinced her that if she didn't try, eventually she would be at risk as well.

Esther felt compelled to go before the king to save the Jews. From how the text is written, we see nothing directly spoken by God. But we don't have to. We see that Esther knew what God wanted her to do.

So what did she do first? She prayed.

She prayed and then fasted for three days.

No food.

No water.

She put on sackcloth. This was serious.

She gave Mordecai a message asking all her people to pray and fast too.

You may be thinking, *I thought the point was not to pray.* No, I never said the point was not to pray at all. It is rather to stop praying and start doing—and that is exactly what Esther did. At the outset of her period of prayer and fasting, she knew: "When this is done, I will go to the king, even though it is against the

71

law. And if I perish, I perish" (Est. 4:16). After three days, she took off the sackcloth, dressed herself in royal attire, and put the plan into action.

There is a time for prayer. Then there is a time for action. Notice that Esther didn't pray about whether or not she should go before the king. She knew that was what she was supposed to do. She was praying that God would move on her behalf and save his people. She was praying for a miracle.

If we are to be faithful to what God has called us to do, there always comes a time of action. It was time to act. Esther got ready to stand before the king. I imagine she went all out in her preparation—as if it were her wedding day plus prom plus the king's ordination ceremony all wrapped into one. Bring on the makeup, the designer dress, the new perfume, the hairstylist, and the Tiffany jewelry. This was no time to mess around. Her only hope was for his first impression to be positive, or else she was dead.

After hours of preparation, she made her way from her side of the palace and stepped through the outer room. She went through the doors and then stood in the doorway of the king's inner room. She said nothing. She stood there, waiting for him to notice. Her heart was most likely beating out of her chest. Her palms were sweating. She hid her fear behind her smile, hoping he wouldn't notice. Her knees were shaking, but thankfully her robes covered them.

Then the king glanced up. He saw her standing there, patiently. He looked her up and down, then peered over to his attendants. No doubt she was wondering if that was it. She knew she hadn't been invited.

With one quick motion he grabbed his golden scepter and extended it in her direction. He welcomed her into his presence. She would live to see another day. Two days later over dinner, she went on to explain the situation and begged the king to intervene on behalf of the Jews.

Haman was soon exposed for the plot and hanged. Mordecai was given the title of advisor to the king, and an edict was sent throughout the empire that the Jews were not to be harmed. Because of Esther's courage and obedience, the lives of all the Jews in the empire were saved. Once she realized that her decision would affect others, she knew she had to act.

A GARDEN PRAYER

There is an instance of this truth in action that affects you directly. It's the most important act ever taken: the cross of Christ. When Christ prayed in the Garden of Gethsemane, he didn't ask for a way out of what God had called him to do. When Jesus asked the Father "may this cup be taken" from him, he was asking if there was another way for God's plan to be put into action (Matt. 26:39). Jesus knew the assignment God had given him: to offer himself as a sacrifice for others. Jesus was willing to die. He was willing to go through with the plan because he knew there was no other way to save humankind. He wasn't trying to get out of God's will; he prayed, "Father, if you are willing, take this cup from me; yet not my will, but yours be done" (Luke 22:42).

After spending time in prayer, Jesus realized it was time to stop praying and start doing. At the end of his prayer, Jesus said, "The hour has come. Look, the Son of Man is delivered into the hands of sinners. Rise! Let us go! Here comes my betrayer!" (Mark 14:41–42).

This is a sign of maturity, and above all, trust. Jesus trusted that God's will was perfect. When we procrastinate, we risk our disobedience affecting others. Much hangs in the balance of our decisions. Can you imagine what the lives of millions of others would be like if Jesus had procrastinated after his prayer? We can be thankful that he thought more about us and his Father than about himself.

WAITING ON PERFECTION

It's easy to procrastinate in prayer by telling God that we'll agree to do what he says as soon as everything aligns perfectly. The myth is that when God calls us to something, every *i* will be dotted and every *t* crossed. We tell ourselves, *If God really wants me to do such-and-such, then clearly all the stars will align.*

This isn't reality, nor is it how God works. God doesn't send a ZIP file with the blueprints of how every single detail in the plan is going to work out. Waiting on perfection is a way for us to justify our inaction. The truth is, when we tack on the stipulations of waiting for every question to be answered before we go, we are being as disobedient as if we'd just said no. Don't let your desire to make wise decisions lead you to procrastinate what God has called you to do.

One of the reasons God calls us to fulfill callings, even

though we don't know how everything will work out, is that our faith in him will grow. God is glorified when we place our faith in him and his provision. Hebrews 11:6 says, "Without faith it is impossible to please God."

Following through with a calling from God when we don't know all the steps requires faith, and this is one of the ways we glorify God with our lives. It's time to stop using prayer as procrastination and start doing what God has called us to do.

CHAPTER 8

YOU ASKED FOR IT

MASKING OUR PRIDE WITH PRAYER ESTRANGES US FROM God. To move beyond this, we need to use our times of prayer to be vulnerable. There's nothing wrong with being scared when God calls you to do something for him, so we need to offer prayers of vulnerability to God, admitting our fears.

But we must not stop there. After admitting our fears, the only way to get past them is to act. The very act of admitting fear to God begins to break the pride from our hearts. First Peter 5:5 says, "God opposes the proud but shows favor to the humble." It takes a humble heart to admit fear, but God has promised to offer grace to the humble. Peter goes on to say that when we humble ourselves, we put ourselves in the position of having God lift us up with his mighty hand (1 Peter 5:6).

Have you ever prayed for something so long that when God finally gave you what you'd been asking for, it paralyzed you with fear? My wife and I prayed and prayed and prayed about having children. Hundreds of others were praying with us and for us. Years went by, and we still had no children.

After we made our decision to adopt, it took a year to process all the paperwork needed to finalize the adoption. During that time, we made changes around the house and turned the home office into a nursery. We had baby showers and stocked up on all the necessities. When the time came for us to travel overseas and bring her home, there was no turning back.

Upon returning home with our baby, we soon discovered the complexities and challenges of being parents. The first few weeks were especially difficult, as we were getting over jet lag and trying to switch our daughter from a twelve-hour time change. With little sleep and little patience, we began to realize that this would be much harder than we'd thought it would be.

In all the years I spent praying for that moment, I never thought I would be fearful once God answered our prayer. Questions ran through my head: *Do I have what it takes to be a good father? How will I meet all my responsibilities? Will we ever sleep again?* Even though the adjustment was much tougher than we realized, we were thrilled to have our daughter. I hadn't thought it was possible to love her as much as I do. To me, this adjustment was a wake-up call; God knows that we'll get overwhelmed by the answers to many of our prayers.

This happened to Moses. He spent forty years thinking about what he would do if he got his shot to go back to Egypt and seek retribution for the slavery of the Israelites. For forty years, he was away from his people's suffering, which he had witnessed with his own eyes. Ready or not, God decided it was time to answer his prayer. God decided he needed a special introduction, so he introduced himself to Moses by using a burning bush that didn't actually burn up. Exodus records the event like this:

> Moses saw that though the bush was on fire it did not burn up. So Moses thought, "I will go over and see this strange sight—why the bush does not burn up."
>
> When the LORD saw that he had gone over to look, God called to him from within the bush, "Moses! Moses!"
>
> And Moses said, "Here I am."
>
> "Do not come any closer," God said. "Take off your sandals, for the place where you are standing is holy ground." Then he said, "I am the God of your father, the God of Abraham, the God of Isaac and the God of Jacob." At this, Moses hid his face, because he was afraid to look at God. . . .
>
> "So now, go. I am sending you to Pharaoh to bring my people the Israelites out of Egypt." (vv. 3:2–6, 10)

Now, here comes the fear:

> But Moses said to God, "Who am I that I should go to Pharaoh and bring the Israelites out of Egypt?" (Ex. 3:11)

"Who am I?" That is a question rooted in fear. *I'm not qualified. I don't have the training. I don't have the experience. I've never done anything like that before.* Moses remembered

79

that the last time he had tried to rescue an Israelite slave, he'd murdered an Egyptian slave master and been driven out of the country. While Moses had been hoping for their rescue, he'd never thought it would come through him.

It's completely understandable that Moses was scared. He was on the Egyptians' most wanted list. He'd fled the scene of a crime and knew CSI could pin the murder on him. Now God wanted him to go back. As if that wasn't enough, Moses wasn't a trained politician. He was a shepherd. He also stuttered when he spoke. How would Pharaoh, or anyone else, take him seriously? After decades of waiting, Moses was finally given his chance, but he was paralyzed by fear.

BACK THERE?

Fear can hold us back from accomplishing what God calls us to do. This doesn't downplay fear or sweep it under the rug as if it doesn't exist. Fear is real and understandable. Overcoming fear is best accomplished by having a proactive prayer life. By strengthening your relationship with the Father, your trust will continue to increase. Trust is the antidote to fear.

Trust is the only thing that could send Elisabeth Elliot back to Ecuador to face the tribe that speared her husband to death. Her fear was real, but so was the call of God.

After months of preparation, Jim Elliot and four other friends set out to make contact with the Waodani tribe living along the Curaray River in Ecuador. Because the Waodani were known to be a tribe of warriors that was violent to outsiders, no missionaries had ever successfully reached them.

Elliot and his friends began making contact via a small plane, which they used to lower gifts in a basket. After months of giving gifts, they decided it was the right time to make physical contact. The pilot, Nate Saint, landed their plane on Palm Beach, where, unknown to the five missionaries, a group of Waodani warriors waited in the woods. On January 8, 1956, all five bodies of the men were found downstream, speared to death. Elliot was survived by his wife, Elisabeth, and ten-month-old daughter, Valerie.

For most people, that would have been all that was necessary for Elisabeth to pack her bags and head home. When the people you're trying to help kill your family, why would you stay? Elisabeth's fear was real. But she was considering the impossible. The only way you stay after pulling your husband out of a river is that you receive a divine calling. The fear she felt was eclipsed by her calling—and her calling was confirmed through her relationship with the Father.

For the next two years, Elisabeth and her infant daughter remained in Ecuador, continuing to minister to the local people. Then, in 1958, Elisabeth answered yes to the crazy call to not only remain in Ecuador but return to the scene of her husband's murder. For two more years, Elisabeth ministered to the Waodani tribe, sharing the good news of the gospel. Through her courageous actions, the Waodani tribe began placing their faith in Jesus. There certainly was fear. But above the fear came the peace of calling.

BREAKING WITH TRADITION

There was a dramatic shift in the life of the early church—a shift that drastically altered its landscape of ministry and influence. For the first years, the apostles focused all their efforts on Israel and the Jews, but that soon changed.

God called Peter to share the gospel with Gentiles, but Peter didn't want to break the law by associating with them. One day, Peter was praying on the roof, waiting on lunch to be made, when he fell into a trance. He was hungry when he fell asleep, so he started dreaming about a buffet like the one from Golden Corral. The problem was, as a Jew, Peter wasn't allowed to eat many items on the buffet.

> He saw heaven opened and something like a large sheet being
> let down to earth by its four corners. It contained all kinds
> of four-footed animals, as well as reptiles and birds. Then a
> voice told him, "Get up, Peter. Kill and eat." (Acts 10:11–13)

A major obstacle between us and our ability to start doing what God wants us to do is our presumption to understand exactly what God is doing and why. Peter responded, "Surely not, Lord! . . . I have never eaten anything impure or unclean" (Acts 10:14). In Peter's response, he was reminding God that there is scripture—in this case, entire books of the Old Testament—that gave him plenty of reasons to object to eating the animals. Peter was saying, "I've been told all my life that I can't eat certain animals because it will separate me from you.

If I eat the animals off the sheet, I'll forfeit my communion with you. You can't possibly expect me to go against what everyone else does!"

Actually, that was exactly what God wanted Peter to do. We must follow God's call over family, church, or cultural tradition. Among the greatest barriers to being radically obedient to God's calling are the expectations of others. Usually this is pressure from your parents, spouse, or close friends. For the person who comes from a family of doctors, going into urban education will be a tough decision for Mom and Dad to swallow. If you're a partner in a successful firm, your partners probably won't be too thrilled with your decision to cash out and start a church. If your mom stayed at home when you were a baby—and so did her mom and her mom's mom before her—she probably expects you to stay home with your baby. But God may have called you to a different life. The fear of disappointment is high. If God has called you to break ranks with others' expectations, don't just pray about it—do it.

Just because the church has always done things one way doesn't mean that it should continue to do so. If Sunday night services have been a tradition for years and are no longer effective, it's okay to end them. Just because everyone in your family is a lawyer doesn't mean you can't be a teacher. If everyone in your family goes to the same university, it doesn't mean you have to as well.

Tradition is never the measuring stick for faithfulness and effectiveness—obeying God is. After Peter pled his case, God answered, "Do not call anything impure that God has made clean" (Acts 10:15). In other words, "Peter, you're ignoring my call and putting too much emphasis on tradition. I've told you to eat, so that should give you enough confidence to do so."

After Peter heard this three times, the sheet was taken back into heaven and Peter woke up from the vision. We soon find out that the vision wasn't just about eating food. It was about Peter's call to share the gospel with Gentiles. Immediately after that, Peter got up and the next phase of the church was born, because he overcame his fear and presumptions about what God had called him to do.

There will be times when God's answer to your prayers brings as much fear as it does joy. If you get the job, it means you have to leave your home. If you get into that school, you won't know anyone. If the grant is awarded to you, you will have to write the book. Fear is always a tension to manage, not a problem to solve. This is why a proactive prayer life is so crucial. Being open with God about your fears will deepen your connection, allowing him to speak peace and truth into your soul. This is how you develop trust with God. Don't be alarmed when fear creeps into your mind. Use it as an opportunity to further engage in your relationship with God.

CHAPTER 9

RELIGIOUS CYCLE LIES

RECENTLY, I HAD THE OPPORTUNITY TO INTERVIEW A PROMInent Christian leader. From the outside, it would seem that her life was pretty good. She and her husband had a great ministry that affected thousands of people. With a thriving ministry, books, and speaking revenues, I imagine they were well-off financially, never worrying about paying the bills. From an outsider's perspective, I was absolutely floored when I heard her say that she was living in the most difficult period of her life. It was a great reminder that how things appear isn't always the way they really are.

On the outside, many people lead similar lives. They seem to have it all together. They seem to have peace. They seem to be so spiritual. But if they were honest, they would tell you that they don't have peace. They don't have the relationship with God that they seem to. And yet, others probably envy them on some level. They think they've got it all together. This is the lie of the Religious Cycle.

As we've seen, the Religious Cycle is all about the external. The focus is on keeping up appearances. This is what happens when we procrastinate, isolate, and allow pride into our lives. We use prayer to procrastinate instead of acting. On the outside, our prayers are praised. We let pride take root because we don't want others to know this side of us. So we isolate ourselves, cutting off others from knowing us beyond the surface.

We cannot find the peace we desire when we only pray about what God has called us to do.

The irony and tragedy is that what those in the Religious Cycle desperately want is exactly what the Religious Cycle cannot deliver. Peace does not come from isolation. Faith that grows does not come from procrastination. Pride does not get us closer to God. The Religious Cycle is a trap; disobedience is baptized in prayer, making it very difficult to effect change.

ANSWER HONESTLY

A distinction needs to be made as we close this section. Please give an honest evaluation of yourself when answering the following questions. The true answers are only known between you and God.

- Do you hear God calling you to do something?
- Are you honestly praying about it?
- What steps have you taken to answer the call?
- Are you using prayer to procrastinate, putting off obedience?

- Are you using prayer to isolate yourself from people who know you?
- Are you really praying, or just pretending?

It's easy to tell people you are praying about selling your business and becoming a missionary. Actually spending time in prayer, though, is difficult.

Believe me, I understand. If we're all honest, sometimes we're scared to hear what he'll say. Sometimes I don't want to pray about what may be next for my family because I know there's a chance it will include a drastic change. And for most people, change is scary.

Regardless of that, the question remains: Are you honestly praying about what God has called you to do? After all, the reason you're not acting on it is because you're still praying about it.

I should mention that sometimes the very action that God has called us to take will be to pray. The kind of prayers I'm calling you to stop praying are the ones you pray to get out of doing something else. Don't take this as a suggestion to stop praying the urgent prayers that God has called you to pray, but also don't let prayer keep you from acting.

But is that really the issue? If you're only claiming to pray when you really aren't, that's the first issue you need to address. When you begin to pray, don't fall into the trap of the Religious Cycle. Don't use prayer as a way to fail to act when God clearly calls you to move.

Are you really praying?

If so, what are you waiting for?

PART 2

START DOING

HOW DO YOU COUNTERACT THE RELIGIOUS CYCLE? HOW DO you stop the spinning? The only way to stop this cycle from spinning is to join the Discipleship Cycle. If you're on the Religious Cycle, it's because you have a reactive prayer life. Your prayers are always reacting to the events in your life. If God brings events into your life that don't make immediate sense, or the timing is longer than expected, you may give up or fail to seize the moment. Think back to the story of Paul in the prison cell. If he hadn't been proactively praying to God, he very well could have missed the entire purpose of his imprisonment.

If you want to join the Discipleship Cycle, you need to develop a proactive prayer life. This means that you are in prayer for the relationship, not just the answers. The more time you spend in proactive prayer, the deeper your relationship with God grows. The deeper your relationship, the deeper the trust. And when you fully trust God, you will not be hindered by prayers when he calls you to do something crazy like start a church or sell the family business. Proactive prayer leads to action. Proactive prayer leads to discipleship. A proactive prayer life will cause you to stop praying when God calls you to act.

The phases of the Discipleship Cycle directly counteract the Religious Cycle. As we will see, saying yes counteracts procrastination, connection counteracts isolation, and selflessness counteracts pride. The remainder of this book will look at each of these phases. If you have a desire to stop praying and actually start doing what God has told you to do, the remaining chapters will help get you there. If there's a nagging idea in your head that you know you should pursue, please keep going. The best time to stop procrastinating is now.

CHAPTER 10

COUNTERACT PROCRASTINATION WITH A YES

WHEN I WAS IN COLLEGE, I LISTENED TO A LOT OF SERMONS BY Louie Giglio. He led a citywide Bible study in Atlanta for many years, and I also heard him speak at a few conferences. One particular thing he said has stuck with me for more than a decade. In discussing a passage of scripture in Isaiah, he came to a verse that said, "Yes, LORD, walking in the way of your laws, we wait for you; your name and renown are the desire of our hearts" (Isa. 26:8). Louie said that the key to having a great relationship with God is found in this verse. If God is really the Lord of our lives, then the only response we can give when he calls is the one Isaiah gave: yes.

If you respond to God with anything but yes, he is not your Lord. "Yes, Lord" is the only response that makes sense. If you say "yes, but," then he is not the Lord of your life. So this is where the Discipleship Cycle starts. It starts with a yes. That yes must be followed by action or it's not really a yes, it's a "yes, but."

To get off the Religious Cycle of procrastination, you must take action. That's what this chapter is about. Sometimes people say yes to huge, crazy calls from God, while others say yes to simple, mundane chores. Many times when God calls us to act, he's more concerned about obedience than he is with the size of the task. Unfortunately, this is one of the main reasons many tasks are ignored—because they're not actions that will receive the attention and recognition we often desire. In one sense, it's completely understandable. Would you rather be remembered as the delivery boy or the superhero? If God is giving us an option, we would most likely all vie to be the superhero. But often the road to saving the day must first be walked as a delivery boy.

THE BOY WHO WOULD BE KING

King David's résumé was pretty impressive (with a few exceptions, as we have seen). He was a military hero. He killed a literal giant without a sword. After victories in battle, the people would line the street and chant his name. He expanded the kingdom of Israel to its largest reach. He killed bears and lions with rocks. He was a man's man. Considering his accomplishments, one would assume that he must have come from an affluent background, where opportunities for learning and achievements were unending.

But that's not the real story. David came from humble beginnings. He was born last of eight sons, at a time when being the oldest was the main ingredient for success. The odds of David succeeding more than his brothers were miniscule. We learn in 1 Samuel 16 that the Lord sent Samuel to find and anoint the next king of Israel. Samuel went to the house of Jesse, David's father. He assumed exactly what everyone else assumed—that he would choose the oldest son. "When they arrived, Samuel saw Eliab and thought, 'Surely the LORD's anointed stands here before the LORD'" (1 Sam. 16:6).

But the Lord told Samuel that Eliab wasn't the one. Jesse called his next six sons to stand before Samuel, who reached the same conclusion. None of these were chosen as king. Samuel asked if there were any other sons, and judging from Jesse's response, it was obvious that not even he thought David would be worthy. "'There is still the youngest,' Jesse answered. 'He is tending the sheep'" (1 Sam. 16:11).

Surely you can't pick the youngest son, Jesse was implying. *He's not old enough. He's not in the army. He's no warrior. He's just tending my sheep. They're not even his own sheep. He's too young to own sheep. Surely, this is a waste of everyone's time.*

If you've ever felt as if you weren't worthy of a task or calling, then take encouragement from what happened next.

> Samuel said, "Send for him; we will not sit down until he arrives."
>
> So [Jesse] sent for him and had him brought in. He was glowing with health and had a fine appearance and handsome features. Then the LORD said, "Rise and anoint him; this is the one." (1 Sam. 16:11–12)

Defying all odds, David was anointed king, chosen over all his brothers.

So Samuel took the horn of oil and anointed him in the presence of his brothers, and from that day on the Spirit of the LORD came powerfully upon David. (1 Sam. 16:13)

This was an easy call to answer for David. "David, do you want to be king?"

"Hmm . . . Let me think about that. Yes!"

We don't see David wrestling in prayer over this decision. Being obedient had never been easier. But what's interesting is what happened immediately following David's anointing. Five verses after Samuel left, David was called to play the harp for Saul, the existing king whom David would one day replace. Can you imagine how David must have felt sitting there, watching Saul sit on his throne each day? He knew he was going to be king, but instead of ruling, he sat at the feet of the existing king playing cover songs on the harp.

Some time later, Israel and Saul were part of a war, so David went back to his old job of tending sheep. David's oldest brothers were allowed to fight with the army, but David remained behind to tend the herds.

How does one stay obedient to God's call when all the tasks at hand seem insulting and below the call of God? Here was David, the next king, and he was working in fields and playing the harp for the current king. How did he remain obedient? He answered with a small yes every time God called. The first small yes was to play the harp. When King Saul summoned him to Jerusalem, David may have thought that his coronation was at hand. Upon arriving into town, however, David learned he was to be on call to play music anytime the king wanted to hear it. Not the welcome David was expecting. So for some amount of time, David continued to go back and forth from tending his father's sheep to playing music for the king he was to one day replace. That was David's life.

During this time, the Israelites went to war with the Philistines, which would be the tipping point for David's career. As the army marched to the battle lines, David as usual was back in the fields, herding sheep. One day, David's father called him in from the fields with an urgent task.

"I need you to go to the battlefront," he said.

David must have been thinking that this was it. His chance had finally arrived! But then his father finished his sentence: ". . . and take this food to your brothers."

David had to be thinking, *You're kidding me!* After he was anointed to be the next king of Israel, all he had done was tend sheep and play the harp, and now he was to be a delivery boy.

But David recognized the principle of the small yes. Saying yes to those small tasks was ultimately what put David in a position to accept the call of God. That's the great benefit of the small yes. David said yes, and this put him in the right place at the right time to fulfill his calling. So David set off with the food for his brothers.

Upon arriving at the battle, David learned that no one was willing to fight the giant Goliath. It's interesting to me that David didn't get overwhelmed with the task, perhaps because it wasn't anything he hadn't seen before. The giant was just like the bear or lion that he had routinely killed in the fields.

So David's small yes to being a shepherd was preparation for his becoming a military hero. David marched down to face the giant, confident that the Lord was with him and that his preparation was enough to win the battle.

The reality is that if David hadn't been obedient with the small yes, he wouldn't have been able to step up and kill Goliath. Had he not killed Goliath, he may not have been catapulted to the top of the army and the entire nation.

A lot hangs in the balance of our small-yes opportunities. Besides seeing David obey the principle of the small yes, we see that he followed with a continued yes. David didn't just say yes once. Anyone can do that. It's easy to show up one Sunday morning to work the nursery, but showing up every week for three years demonstrates commitment. It's easy to go to the gym once, but going three or four times a week for months takes work. That's what we see with David. He continued to be obedient to the menial tasks that God put before him. The continued yes is essential for long-term success and faithful obedience.

Maybe you can relate to David. Maybe you feel called to slay giants, but you spend your time being a delivery boy. Maybe you feel called to be the CEO, but you work in the mailroom. Maybe you want to be the senior pastor, but you're working part-time with the youth group. Maybe you want to run the restaurant, but you're washing dishes. Take encouragement from David's story. By doing the menial tasks, you are setting yourself up to one day fulfill your calling.

HE SAID YES TWENTY TIMES

The Discipleship Cycle is about saying yes, yes, yes, and yes again. This is not only the cycle of discipleship; it's also the cycle of world change. Sometimes saying yes nineteen times in nineteen years to the same call isn't enough; sometimes it takes twenty yeses to accomplish what you're called to do.

That was the story of William Wilberforce. For twenty years as a member of Parliament, he fought to end the transatlantic slave trade in Great Britain. And for nineteen years, it was voted down. Over the course of those twenty years, the fight cost Wilberforce his health, reputation, time, and wealth. He was repeatedly disappointed by friends who promised to support his bill, only to back out at the last moment because of a bribe. He was lied about in the press. He received constant death threats. He nearly died numerous times and suffered from ulcerative colitis and other illnesses brought on by fatigue.[1]

But every year, he said yes to his calling. Every year, he continued the fight to end the slave trade. And if he had stopped after nineteen years, he would have failed. On the twentieth year, however, he said yes one more time, and that time he won.[2] He continually said yes, and in the end his obedience led to the freedom of millions of people.

Saying yes cost him his health, reputation, and time, but ultimately he received the peace that can only be achieved by living in the Discipleship Cycle.

SAINT PATRICK

Every March, millions of people around the world dress up in green sparkly hats, glasses, shirts, and other ridiculous garb to celebrate the life of Saint Patrick, a man they most likely know very little about. Irish pubs overflow, rivers are dyed green, and Guinness flows from an everlasting tap, all in the name of a man from the fourth century who wasn't even Irish. Patrick grew up in a Christian home, a churchgoer whose faith was nominal at best. Not much in his life at that point was saint-worthy. But at the age of sixteen, everything changed when he was kidnapped by Irish raiders.

For the next six years, British-born Patrick worked in the fields of western Ireland as a slave tending sheep for his master. Alone and isolated, Patrick's faith began to deepen and grow in unexpected ways.

> God used the time to shape and mold me into something better. He made me into what I am now—someone very different from what I was, someone who can care about others and work to help them. Before I was a slave, I didn't even care about myself.[3]

He spent his time saying up to one hundred prayers a day. Some of his prayers have been preserved, including the famous Breastplate Prayer and the Prayer of Protection:

> *As I arise today,*
> *may the strength of God pilot me,*

the power of God uphold me,
the wisdom of God guide me.
May the eye of God look before me,
the ear of God hear me,
the word of God speak for me.
May the hand of God protect me,
the way of God lie before me,
the shield of God defend me,
the host of God save me.
May Christ shield me today.
Christ with me, Christ before me,
Christ behind me,
Christ in me, Christ beneath me,
Christ above me,
Christ on my right, Christ on my left,
Christ when I lie down, Christ when I sit,
Christ when I stand,
Christ in the heart of everyone who thinks of me,
Christ in the mouth of everyone who speaks of me,
Christ in every eye that sees me,
Christ in every ear that hears me.
Amen.[4]

Patrick's faith grew to where his understanding and trust in God moved beyond his circumstances. His desire was to be obedient where God had placed him, even in slavery. The last four verses of his prayer speak of his desire to have Christ reflected in his every interaction with people, even those who had brutally held him captive. His growing trust in God would lead to

his ability to make seemingly foolish decisions from an outside perspective, but because Patrick was in the Discipleship Cycle, he was able to move forward in confidence.

After six years of slavery, Patrick had a vision that his freedom was waiting for him on the eastern coast of Ireland. Traveling through the night, Patrick boarded a ship home to Britain. His freedom was short-lived, as he was once again sold into slavery, this time in France. After some time, he received a second vision of how to escape and was safely reunited with his family. Upon returning, his family asked him to swear never to leave them again.

After years of slavery, Patrick was enjoying the comforts and safety of home when he received another vision. His former captors were asking their holy servant boy to return to them and shepherd them. His family pleaded with him to stay, but around AD 432, he took his inheritance and willingly sailed back to Ireland without a formal ecclesiastical sanction. Legend says he drove all the snakes out of Ireland and explained the Trinity using a shamrock. More importantly, Patrick spent the remaining thirty years of his life influencing the entire country of Ireland. He helped start new churches, shared the gospel with tribes, taught literacy, and provided leadership for churches throughout the region. His work prepared the way for the great Irish revival that started in the sixth century.[5]

Patrick was willing to answer the crazy call of returning to Ireland because of his deep relationship with God. His proactive prayer life led to a strong connection with his heavenly Father that enabled him to respond with a bold yes when everyone around him wanted him to say no. Imagine your entire family begging you to say no to a call you felt was from God. From the outside, the Discipleship Cycle may look foolish, but when you believe that Christ is with you, Christ before you, Christ behind you, Christ in you, Christ beneath you, Christ above you, Christ on your right, and Christ on your left, you have confidence to say yes.

THE REALITIES OF THE CYCLE

From the outside, the Discipleship Cycle is a bit crazy. Unless someone is living in it, there's almost no way to understand what you're doing and why you're doing it. Those living in the Religious Cycle would never admit it, but they are probably jealous. What they want so badly, they cannot receive because of their pride. They want peace. They want a vivacious faith. They want a life that makes an eternal impact. But these are impossible while living in the Religious Cycle.

What the Religious Cycle promises on the outside is exactly what the Discipleship Cycle provides on the inside: peace. Ironically, the isolation people feel on the inside in the Religious Cycle is manifested on the outside in the Discipleship Cycle. Wilberforce is a good example of this. His friends deserted him on many occasions, he was ostracized by his peers, and he was ridiculed in the press. Yet in his isolation he had peace because he kept saying yes.

CHAPTER 11
COUNTERACT ISOLATION WITH COMMUNITY

WHAT WOULD YOU DO IF YOUR LIFE DEPENDED ON OUTLASTING your neighbor, if survival meant doing anything you could to stay ahead of those around you? What would you do if the only way you could eat was to ensure the man beside you didn't? Ernest Gordon found himself in this trap. The only rules were "It's every man for himself" and "Look out for number one." It was all about survival and doing whatever was necessary to make it one more day. Some days it meant stealing from a neighbor the only cup of rice he would get all day. Sometimes it meant rummaging for valuables on dead bodies to have something to sell on the black market for medicine or cigarettes. This was no place to love your neighbor as yourself. Gordon, like thousands of other soldiers, was trapped in a Japanese POW camp.

For those misfortunate enough to wind up in a German or Italian POW camp during World War II, roughly 96 percent made it out alive. Sadly, this does not include those forced into concentration camps. In comparison, the survival rate falls to 73 percent when you look at the Japanese POW camps. It was even worse for those who were forced to work on the River Kwai, where the number of survivors was lower still.[1]

Ernest Gordon, however, learned that survival would ultimately mean looking out for others more than himself. The three and a half years he spent as a "guest" of the Japanese army would radically change his understanding of faith, hope, and love.

"In the beginning," Gordon recalled, "morale in the camp was low, especially among the officers."[2] Most prisoners had recently been captured, and many had seen or heard of the Japanese killing soldiers and citizens, later to be deemed massacred.

> Another factor that contributed to low morale was the insufficiency of our diet. The basic ration was rice amounting to less than twelve ounces per man per day. Meat, flour, sugar, and salt were provided in such small amounts that they were hardly worth mentioning. The rice was highly polished and therefore contained none of the essential vitamins, proteins, or minerals. The immediate results of this starvation diet were hunger, general depression and blackouts. Next came the host of diseases caused by vitamin deficiency—such as beriberi and pellagra.[3]

Conditions were obviously bad, but they would only get worse when the physical labor started. Within weeks, Gordon and others were taken by train into Thailand to begin work on a Japanese supply railroad. The plan originally called for eighteen months to complete construction. However, when inclement weather delayed the start for six months, the Japanese decided the original deadline still had to be met.[4]

For the next year, an estimated thirteen thousand prisoners of war died while building the railroad. This pales in comparison to the eighty to a hundred thousand enslaved civilians who also died. Seven days a week, workers would rise before dawn and work past dark, hacking through dense jungle forest with only hand tools. Most wore only loincloths and worked barefooted as temperatures rose to 120 degrees Fahrenheit. If they slowed down, workers were beaten and many killed on the spot. More and more men fell into starvation and malnutrition. To make matters worse, sick men weren't allotted food. Rice was only available to men who worked.

> As conditions steadily worsened, as starvation, exhaustion and disease took an ever-increasing toll, the atmosphere in which we lived became poisoned by selfishness, hate and fear. We were slipping rapidly down the slope of degradation.[5]

Everyday, people were dying. To avoid being next, the prisoners would do whatever was necessary to stay alive. This meant stealing other people's bags of rice while they slept, or bribing the person who distributed the rice.

Deceit and selfishness were the only rules—and it started to become evident to Gordon and others that it wasn't working.

Although we lived by the law of the jungle, the strongest among us still died, and the most selfish, the most self-sufficient, the wiliest and shrewdest, perished with the weak, the generous and the decent.[6]

But like the changing seasons, there began a gradual change in Gordon that would soon sweep through the entire camp and alter the trajectory of his life. After battling many illnesses, Gordon found himself in the "death house," as he had been diagnosed with polyneuritis and could no longer use his legs. The death house was a shed where sick prisoners were left to die, isolated from other prisoners to contain their diseases from spreading throughout the camp. There was little that could be done for Gordon, and the Japanese had written him off. Even the British medical officer in the camp saw little hope of his recovery. But with the help of some friends, Gordon left the death house to live in a one-man shelter they had built for him.

Over the course of the next few weeks and months, some new friends came by daily to help Gordon regain the use of his legs, which were covered with ulcers, pus, and sores from infection. His friends would wash and massage his legs every day to help restore blood flow. This sacrificial act restored Gordon to health when everyone had written him off.

He regained his ability to walk. During this time, Gordon began to investigate the truths of Christ. After seeing the gospel in action, it became evident that there was hope even when surrounded by death.

Gordon began leading meetings to discuss the life and teachings of Christ. While he did admit that he didn't have all the answers, he engaged the process with much enthusiasm and passion. Soon, men began to live out their faith. People began serving the sick and dying, as Gordon's friends had done for him. Men who once stole just to get a few more ounces of rice now voluntarily gave up entire meals to those who were dying. The mood of the entire camp began to change.

> Generosity proved to be contagious. Once begun, this charity soon extended beyond regimental loyalties to include any man in need. Men started thinking less of themselves, of their own discomforts and plans, and more of their responsibilities to others. Although the pay which the other ranks had to share was even less than that of the officers, they, too, found ways to give expression to their generous impulses.[7]

Now, I love this next part:

> It was dawning on us all—officers and other ranks alike—that the law of the jungle is not the law of man. We had seen for ourselves how quickly it could strip most of us of our humanity and reduce us to levels lower than beasts.[8]

For the remainder of his time as a POW, Gordon helped lead a Christian movement in the prison camps. Many men came to see the truth of Christianity, mainly through the lives of men living their faith in the worst circumstances humanly possible. When men began to lay down their own lives for the sake of others, monumental change occurred.

If ever there was a time when turning the other cheek could

have been forgotten, certainly being a POW was it. When every day was a fight to stay alive, certainly that was the time to look out for number one. That wasn't what Gordon and his friends decided to do. They decided to take the commands of Jesus literally and obey them. They chose to serve others, including their enemies. They voluntarily gave up their small rations of food to help revive the dying.

What's fascinating about Gordon's memoir is the minimal mention of prayer. He doesn't mention any moments of praying about whether he should serve his fellow prisoners. He doesn't mention praying about whether to wash the sores of men who were too weak to do it themselves. It was obvious to Gordon that just praying about a starving friend was pointless if he wouldn't help by giving what he could. The story of the POW camps in Thailand during World War II is remembered for those who acted out their faith.

EVEN THE GREATEST DOUBT

When we live in community, we have opportunities that isolation prohibits. Opportunities to serve are impossible in isolation, but they flourish in community. In community, you can express your doubts with the hope of encouragement to continue through dark times. Ernest Gordon had doubts that were answered through community. Had he continued his isolation, he would have withered away unnoticed in a jungle prison. Community counteracts isolation and is essential for fighting through difficult times.

Jesus called John the Baptist the greatest man born among

women (Matt. 11:11). Think about that for a moment. That's an honor far greater than any Nobel Prize, Oscar, Emmy, or MTV Music Award. John had a thriving ministry. He was bold with his faith. He stood up to the Pharisees in a time when few would.

Near the peak of his ministry, John had a revelation. His purpose was to prepare the way for the Messiah. When he saw Jesus walk by, he openly declared that this was the Son of God (John 1:29–34). Some of his disciples left him to follow Jesus. Still others stayed behind, remaining an integral part of John's ministry.

After years of fruitful ministry, John the Baptist found himself in an impossible predicament. His ministry was taken from him and he was thrown in jail, awaiting the death penalty. He was isolated from his community. Alone in a prison cell, he started doubting everything he thought he understood.

> When John, who was in prison, heard about the deeds of the Messiah, he sent his disciples to ask him, "Are you the one who is to come, or should we expect someone else?"
>
> Jesus replied, "Go back and report to John what you hear and see: The blind receive sight, the lame walk, those who have leprosy are cleansed, the deaf hear, the dead are raised, and the good news is proclaimed to the poor. Blessed is anyone who does not stumble on account of me." (Matt. 11:2–6)

In his isolation, John wanted confirmation that Jesus was who he said he was. For John, life had gotten very difficult. He had questions. Serious questions. Events were happening that didn't line up. This happens to all of us. A friend gets sick, a parent dies, a job is lost—something unexpected disrupts our lives. Most of us, like John, are doing our best to follow God's call, so when these events happen, it's understandable that we would doubt our paths.

Community won't take away our pain or prevent difficult events. What it will do is provide you with the needed support and encouragement to work through them. Jesus had to remind John of the good that was still happening. It may have been difficult to see, but God was still working. The blind were seeing. The lame were walking. The lepers were healed. The deaf could hear. The dead were raised. Jesus wanted John to know that the good news was being preached to the poor. God was still moving.

If John the Baptist had doubts, then we will too. Isolation breeds doubt, and doubt makes it difficult to act.

RELIGIOUS VERSUS SPIRITUAL

The growing trend of the last decade among young, evangelical Christians is that they want to avoid being known as religious. Rather, their desire is to be spiritual. Why? Because being religious is branded with hypocrisy, blowing up buildings, burning sacred books, and screaming at people leaving abortion clinics. In our new world of relativity, religion is tainted. So, those desiring to rid themselves of that image have shifted toward being spiritual, and in this shift the idea of doing works has been deemed religious.

This attempt at pure spirituality has caused more damage

than many anticipated. The idea of works is essential to any relationship—which is at the heart of Christianity. God has always desired to connect with his people. From the garden of Eden, to the establishment of the nation of Israel, to the sending of Christ to be the atoning sacrifice for our sins, his goal has been all about establishing a relationship—and you can't have a relationship without works, effort, and time.

But the works don't establish the relationship; they further it and define it. You don't show up at someone's door with flowers and pay for her dinner unless you're dating her. The flowers don't establish the relationship, but they help define it. Guys, if you're dating someone but you never pay for dinner, bring her flowers, or do something for her to show your feelings, then those actions will serve to define the relationship (while there still is one). Our actions reveal the reality and depth of our relationships.

When Jesus got up before sunrise to spend time with the Father, he did it to further their relationship. When he spent time with Scripture, it wasn't to establish the relationship but to define it.

Paul spent consistent time in prayer and study. He was disciplined in the way he did evangelism. He did works. Jesus did works too. The leaders of the church for the past two thousand years have done works. Why would we think we should be any different now?

In our efforts to avoid a mechanical religion, we've forgotten that all relationships take work, and our works are a response to those relationships.

CHAPTER 12
COUNTERACT PRIDE WITH SELFLESSNESS

THE THIRD PHASE OF THE RELIGIOUS CYCLE IS DANGEROUS because pride is incredibly difficult to defeat. Given our sinful nature, the preservation of our own desires always hovers near the surface. The primary characteristic of pride is concern for self. We are concerned with how we are perceived, so we hold back. We are concerned with how we perform, so we fudge the numbers. We are concerned with what our church friends think about us, so we tell them we are praying to keep them from prodding any deeper. Pride keeps our primary focus on ourselves, which makes getting off the Religious Cycle extremely difficult. So how do we slay the dragon of pride?

The best starting point is to serve others. When we serve others, we put them ahead of ourselves, taking the attention off our own needs and desires. In Scripture, there are three distinct ways to achieve this: compassion, grace, and humility. In these ways we serve others through words, thoughts, and actions. Each one is a choice while at the same time a posture of our hearts. Let's spend some time looking at each one.

COMPASSION

Jesus shared an interesting parable toward the end of his ministry, which Matthew recorded in his gospel. Jesus said that when he comes back in his glory, he will be attended by angels while sitting on his heavenly throne. All the peoples of the earth will be gathered together and then separated as sheep and goats. The sheep will be rewarded, while the goats will be punished.

Jesus will say this to the sheep:

> Then the King will say to those on his right, "Come, you who are blessed by my Father; take your inheritance, the kingdom prepared for you since the creation of the world. For I was hungry and you gave me something to eat, I was thirsty and you gave me something to drink, I was a stranger and you invited me in, I needed clothes and you clothed me, I was sick and you looked after me, I was in prison and you came to visit me." (Matt. 25:34–36)

The sheep seem to be confused. They ask Jesus when they ever performed these acts of compassion toward him. He will reply, "Truly I tell you, whatever you did for one of the least of these brothers and sisters of mine, you did for me" (Matt. 25:40).

Throughout the gospels, we find Jesus modeling a life of compassion. He was continually giving compassion to those around him by healing diseases, casting out demons, and meeting people's physical needs. As his ministry grew, so did the crowds. But this didn't affect his desire and ability to give compassion. Matthew recorded it this way:

Jesus went through all the towns and villages, teaching in their synagogues, proclaiming the good news of the kingdom and healing every disease and sickness. When he saw the crowds, he had compassion on them, because they were harassed and helpless, like sheep without a shepherd. (Matt. 9:35–36)

When I am surrounded by a huge crowd, like sitting in traffic on the beltway in DC or walking to a football game at Death Valley on Clemson University's campus, my first thoughts—usually of frustration and contempt—are how to get out of the crowd, how to avoid it. These people are keeping me from getting to where I want to go. My last thought is compassion.

But this wasn't so with Jesus. He was able to look past the sheer size of the crowd and see people's individual needs. Mark recorded an event like this:

During those days another large crowd gathered. Since they had nothing to eat, Jesus called his disciples to him and said, "I have compassion for these people; they have already been with me three days and have nothing to eat. If I send them home hungry, they will collapse on the way, because some of them have come a long distance." (Mark 8:1–3)

Jesus had compassion on the people in his life. Later, the early church was taught to continue extending compassion to those in their lives. To Paul, compassion was an expected extension of a life that had been redeemed by Christ. He wrote,

"Be kind and compassionate to one another, forgiving each other, just as in Christ God forgave you" (Eph. 4:32). He wrote further, "Therefore, as God's chosen people, holy and dearly loved, clothe yourselves with compassion, kindness, humility, gentleness and patience" (Col. 3:12). Jesus modeled a life of compassion in how he lived and ministered to those in need.

But it was in his death that he showed the ultimate act of compassion—and this is our example to follow.

GRACE

When we fail to extend grace to those who have offended us, it's because we have forgotten the depth of our sin and the depth of Christ's love to forgive us. The message of the gospel is that we received the forgiveness we didn't deserve because Christ died the death he didn't deserve. When we begin to frame our lives and circumstances through that understanding, our abilities to forgive and extend grace dramatically increase.

I don't know you, your life, or your circumstances. I'm sure that some of you have experienced terrible events in your past. These hurts are very real and deep. I know the effects of alcohol, abuse, and neglect, and there are further pains beyond those that many of you have lived or are in the middle of living right now.

My point is not that you should disregard your past. My hope is to reframe it in light of the gospel, for only when we see the depth of the forgiveness we have received will we be willing to offer it in return. Paul wrote,

As for you, you were dead in your transgressions and sins. . . .
But because of his great love for us, God, who is rich in mercy,
made us alive with Christ even when we were dead in transgressions—it is by grace you have been saved. (Eph. 2:1, 4–5)

Paul couldn't have spelled it out more clearly. We are all
sinners separated from God, and if it wasn't for his grace and forgiveness, we would be separated forever. But it wasn't a matter of
God just saying, "I forgive you." Forgiveness always costs something, and for God, it cost the suffering and death of his Son.

This is the reason we can offer forgiveness and grace to
those who have wronged us. Forgiving others as Christ forgave
us is the command we are to follow. We don't have to pray about
whether or not we should forgive. The answer is always yes. And
this means forgiveness without strings attached.

GENEROSITY

If you have a choice between being generous or greedy, it is safe
to assume that generosity is the way to go. Jesus said,

So when you give to the needy, do not announce it with
trumpets, as the hypocrites do in the synagogues and on the
streets, to be honored by others. Truly I tell you, they have
received their reward in full. But when you give to the needy,
do not let your left hand know what your right hand is doing,
so that your giving may be in secret. (Matt. 6:2–4)

GREG DARLEY

Did you see the assumption in what Jesus said? He didn't say, "If you give to the poor" or "I think you should give to the poor." Jesus assumed that his listeners knew they were supposed to be generous. He said, "*When* you give to the needy." The real instruction in this passage is the way Jesus described how the giving should take place. He was more concerned with the heart of the giver. Our desire should be to be generous, not to receive recognition. The heart of the gospel is that Jesus was generous. He gave up everything to redeem his people. Because of his generosity, Jesus expects us to be generous to others. This is something you don't have to pray about.

When I started my first nonprofit ministry a few years ago, I met with a great leader who was a very successful fundraiser. I wanted to learn how he had raised millions of dollars for his ministry. One of the most important lessons he taught me was to always walk away from a fund-raising meeting with referrals of friends who could also become donors. Taking his advice to heart, I immediately asked him for the names of some friends who would connect with the vision of our ministry. I'm not sure if he was expecting that or not, but he said he would e-mail me a few names and contact information the following week.

"One of these guys you will immediately like," he told me.

"Why's that?" I asked.

"Because he gives to every single person who asks him for help."

"Wow! Is he a millionaire?"

"No. He just takes generosity seriously. He may only give you twenty dollars, but I guarantee he will give you something."

Generosity is not limited to your wallet. There are plenty of ways you can be generous that don't directly involve money. You can be generous with your time by volunteering in the community, helping a neighbor with some yard work, or helping with chores around the house. You can also be generous with your stuff. Let a friend borrow your car when his is in the shop. Invite people over for dinner, and make sure they bring nothing but an appetite. Being generous is more than a transaction, but it must begin there.

HUMILITY

A few years ago, I had the privilege of interviewing the late Chuck Colson for a ministry event. It was a moment I will never forget. If you've spent any time with me or read any of my other writings, odds are you've heard me talk about Chuck. He's had a tremendous impact on me—my thinking, theology, and ministry. I owe him a debt of gratitude that I'll never be able to pay back.

Chuck is a man of amazing accomplishments, both individually and with the organization he led. He is the author of more than thirty books and has fifteen honorary doctorate degrees. He was awarded the Templeton Prize in 1993, with a one-million-dollar grant, the largest award for service in religion. He also founded Prison Fellowship in 1976, which has since grown to be the largest prison ministry in the world, working in prisons in more than 112 countries.

As I was getting ready for my interview with Chuck, I had a lot of questions. Some other young leaders were also going to participate in the interview with some Q&A. In the opening minutes, Chuck gave a quick overview of his ministry and the heart of his teaching. As he passionately described why he cared so much about restoring the justice system, he mentioned many different studies, professors, books, and articles to prove his point. He quoted many researchers, with names I could barely pronounce, much less spell. And he did all this without reading anything. He had no notes.

When the Q&A started, a young pastor from Philadelphia asked this question: "Chuck, with all the responsibilities you have, including writing books, traveling, speaking, and leading a multimillion-dollar organization, how do you balance your time to still give your family and friends the time they deserve?"

Great question. I was wondering the same thing. His answer was one of the best leadership lessons I have ever learned.

Chuck took a deep breath and said, "I'm actually really bad at time management," he said. "Luckily I have a very forgiving wife. I'm really not the person to answer that question. I know there are much better people you can ask. Sorry."

I have thought and talked about that answer dozens of times since. Here was a man who counseled presidents, dined with dignitaries, and was Ivy League educated. He accomplished more than most ever dream possible. The reality is, he could have said anything and everyone listening would have written it down and tried to implement it in their own lives. If Chuck Colson had said he knew the best way to manage your time, we'd all be listening. But he didn't do that.

In his answer, I saw a genuine humility that is so rare in

leaders of his caliber. I also learned that humility is something you don't need to pray about. Paul tells us that our attitudes should be the same as Christ Jesus':

> Do nothing out of selfish ambition or vain conceit. Rather, in humility value others above yourselves, not looking to your own interests but each of you to the interests of the others.
>
> In your relationships with one another, have the same mindset as Christ Jesus:

Who, being in very nature God,
did not consider equality with God some-
thing to be used to his own
advantage;
rather, he made himself nothing
by taking the very nature of a servant,
being made in human likeness.
And being found in appearance as a man,
he humbled himself
by becoming obedient to death—even death on a cross!
(Phil. 2:3–8)

In every circumstance, we are called to be humble. This is honestly one of the hardest commands of Scripture for me to consistently obey. I have a strong, visionary personality, which is a nice way to say that I assume I'm always right. The words *I don't know* have been absent from my vocabulary for decades. But in that moment listening to Chuck, I learned that admitting that I didn't know wasn't a sign of weakness, but of humility.

121

Peter wrote that there is also something else at work when we are prideful:

> In the same way, you who are younger, submit yourselves to your elders. All of you, clothe yourselves with humility toward one another, because,
>
> > *"God opposes the proud*
> > *but shows favor to the humble."*
>
> Humble yourselves, therefore, under God's mighty hand, that he may lift you up in due time. (1 Peter 5:5–6)

Did you catch the significance of what Peter said there? He said that when we're prideful, God opposes us. This means he is literally trying to stop us from accomplishing what we desire. There are a lot of people whom I wouldn't want opposing my plans, but God is clearly at the top of that list. I don't think we need any more reasons to see that humility is something we don't need to pray about.

THE FIRST STEP

Keep in mind that this was a starting point. There are additional commands from Scripture that we need to follow. Becoming a disciple of Christ involves more than a handful of actions, but it starts there. Along the path of discipleship, we know there are many times when we shouldn't pause to pray—instead, we are called to act. Continually acting out of obedience in these areas will lead to greater faith, trust, and worship of God.

It takes continual focus to counteract the pride in our own hearts. When we start believing we don't need to serve others or extend grace to those who fail us, we allow pride to gain a footing in our souls. Pride then tells us we don't need anyone, including God, in our lives. These lies affect our thinking and our decisions. The Religious Cycle is common among prideful people who don't want to admit their need of others and choose to serve only their own interests.

Jesus told a parable near the end of his ministry that described what would happen when everyone stood before the Father to be judged. His words are chilling:

> When the Son of Man comes in his glory, and all the angels with him, he will sit on his glorious throne. All the nations will be gathered before him, and he will separate the people one from another as a shepherd separates the sheep from the goats. He will put the sheep on his right and the goats on his left.
>
> Then the King will say to those on his right, "Come, you who are blessed by my Father; take your inheritance, the kingdom prepared for you since the creation of the world. For I was hungry and you gave me something to eat, I was thirsty and you gave me something to drink, I was a stranger and you invited me in, I needed clothes and you clothed me, I was sick and you looked after me, I was in prison and you came to visit me."
>
> Then the righteous will answer him, "Lord, when did

we see you hungry and feed you, or thirsty and give you something to drink? When did we see you a stranger and invite you in, or needing clothes and clothe you? When did we see you sick or in prison and go to visit you?"

The King will reply, "Truly I tell you, whatever you did for one of the least of these brothers and sisters of mine, you did for me." (Matt. 25:31–40)

Serving others is a distinguishing mark of those in the Discipleship Cycle. Jesus said that when we serve the least of those in society, we are directly serving him. One of the great ironies is that Jesus desires us to be humble and to serve others. Yet the only way you can truly serve someone is through humility. By being obedient to our call to serve "the least of these," we will in turn counteract the pride in our lives, allowing humility to come inside.

CHAPTER 13

LISTEN FOR THE NUDGE

TO CONTINUE OBEDIENTLY IN THE DISCIPLESHIP CYCLE, YOU have to keep saying yes. Sometimes it will be the same yes over and over again. Parents, patience will probably be your continued yes. If you have a boss who's a jerk, respect will be your continued yes. But what do you do when there's no yes to respond to? What do you do when you're genuinely saying yes to everything God calls you to? Listen for the nudge.

A nudge from God is usually small. It's not loud. You'll have to truly focus in order to hear it. Sometimes a nudge only comes once. Other times nudges will continue until you respond. A nudge can be as subtle as a feeling that you should say thank you to a cashier, or as bold as finally apologizing to an ex-spouse you haven't spoken to in years. One of the common threads I'm learning about the nudges from God is that they mainly focus on action. When God nudges, he wants me to do something for him—to be proactive.

PAUL'S NUDGE

For most of Paul's ministry, he went to different towns preaching the gospel and starting churches. His goal was to go where he knew the gospel had never been preached before. Many times, the length of time he stayed in one place was determined by the events happening in his current town. But other times, God nudged Paul exactly where he was to go.

After Timothy joined Paul's team, they traveled around Phrygia and Galatia preaching and encouraging the believers there. In Acts 16, Luke tells us how their steps were determined. He said that the Holy Spirit stopped them from preaching the Word in Asia.

> When they came to the border of Mysia, they tried to enter Bithynia, but the Spirit of Jesus would not allow them to. So they passed by Mysia and went down to Troas. (vv. 7–8)

This shows us that even when we desire to do things for God, sometimes the timing isn't right, so God stops us—or better, he tells us to wait. But notice what Paul didn't do. He didn't pout or get mad. He didn't throw his stuff down and refuse to keep going. Paul took it in stride and continued on to the next town. I believe it was because of this obedience that God opened the door for him to preach where he had recently been unable to, for that very night Paul received the call from God to preach in Macedonia. "During the night Paul had a vision of a man of Macedonia standing and begging him, 'Come over to Macedonia and help us'" (Acts 16:9).

Paul was rewarded for his obedience, and his response was exactly what God was looking for. "After Paul had seen the vision, we got ready at once to leave for Macedonia, concluding that God had called us to preach the gospel to them" (Acts 16:10).

I doubt Paul cared if he woke everyone up in the middle of the night. Being a traveling speaker in those days was no easy job. The terrain was rough and included a lot of walking. I'm sure most of his companions were enjoying their rest when Paul turned on all the candles and woke them up, saying, "Get up! Pack all your stuff. We're leaving!"

"Where are we going?"

"We're going to Macedonia."

"But I thought we weren't allowed to go there. Remember what happened yesterday?"

"Yes, but the Lord has now opened the door and we're leaving."

I love that about Paul. God opened the door, and Paul wasn't going to see how long it would remain open. He decided to go immediately—in the middle of the night. I wonder if Paul ever even unpacked his stuff, or if he was in a constant state of preparation, ready to move at a moment's notice. When God nudges and opens a way, we must be ready to respond—immediately.

I HONESTLY DON'T KNOW WHAT TO DO

I went through a season a few years ago when God was eerily quiet. When I prayed for direction or insight, there was nothing but silence. The conversations typically went like this. Maybe you can relate.

> **ME:** God? What do you think I should do?
>
> **GOD:** (silence)
>
> **ME:** God, I really want to do your will. Can you tell me what that is?
>
> **GOD:** (the sound of crickets)
>
> **ME:** God, will you give me clarity on what I should be doing?
>
> **GOD:** (more silence)
>
> **ME:** God? Are you even listening? I can't hear you. Will you answer me?

Day after day, the conversations continued in the same fashion. I would ask God for an answer on a decision, and in return I would hear nothing. I was at a crossroads and honestly didn't know what God wanted me to do. I prayed. I sought counsel. I prayed more. God was incredibly silent.

Early one Saturday morning, I snuck away before anyone in my house was awake and went to a favorite spot in downtown Greenville. The Reedy River cuts through downtown and cascades down multiple waterfalls. At the top of the falls are numerous benches and tables. I love to watch the sun rise above the falls and enjoy the quiet of the morning while reading and drinking a latte from a local coffee shop.

As I was reading the Bible that Saturday, I was again struck with the frustration of not knowing what God wanted me to do. I prayed, *God, I really want to do your will. And I will do it, but first I need to know what it is.* I mean, how could

God expect me to do his will if he wasn't telling me what it was, right?

As I was praying and reading, I was struck by a simple word from the Lord. It was great on the one hand, because it was the first time in months I'd felt anything fresh from God. But it was frustrating on the other hand because it was nowhere near the level of detail I desired. God reminded me on the bench overlooking the waterfall that he had already given me many insights into his will. In fact, I was currently reading part of his will for my life.

In front of me, my Bible was open to the book of Philippians. I continued reading, but this time the words on the page jumped out at me. I heard God say, "You want to know what I want you to do? Start by being obedient to what I've already commanded you. I've given you a lot to do. I want you to have my attitude and mind-set. I want your life to look like mine."

I looked down and read Philippians 2:14—"Do everything without grumbling or arguing." It was like an explosion of dynamite. In an instant, God's Word busted through the fog of silence. God had spoken clearly about what he desired from my life. I kept reading and wrote down all the actions and commands I could implement in my life, along with the corresponding scriptures. After a few minutes of reading and writing, I had pages of decisions and actions I knew would take a long time to implement. I was overcome with joy that God had spoken!

Here are a few of the entries I wrote in my journal:

- Imitate him (Eph. 5:1).
- Think about what is pure, holy, and right (Phil. 4:8).

- Be joyful (1 Thes. 5:16).
- Pray continually (1 Thes. 5:17).
- Give thanks in all circumstances (1 Thes. 5:18).
- Let the word of Christ dwell in me (Col. 3:17).
- Be kind to the poor (Prov. 19:17).
- Focus my heart on heavenly things (Col. 3:2).
- Be kind and compassionate (Eph. 4:32).
- Be devoted in prayer (Col. 4:2).
- Live above reproach (1 Tim. 3:2).
- Make the most of every opportunity (Col. 4:5).

I spent the next few mornings doing the same exercise—reading through Scripture and writing down the things God wanted to be present in my life. I stopped after writing seventy-four entries, knowing that I had plenty to work on, for God had clearly spoken.

Then something interesting happened. I had been frustrated with God for so long, but when I read back through my list, I realized I wasn't coming close to living out what was there. Was I really imitating him? Was I always thinking about what was pure, holy, and right? I was joyful sometimes, if you didn't count being stuck in traffic, waiting in slow lines at the airport, and paying the bills. I wasn't praying every day, much less continually. I honestly couldn't even comprehend the thought of giving thanks in all circumstances. I was thankful sometimes, but in everything? That didn't make any sense. How was I being kind to the poor? Was I living above reproach and making the most of every opportunity?

After my quick self inventory, I realized that my issue was

not *not* hearing from God; my issue was being obedient to what God had clearly spoken, for all these commands were part of me fulfilling God's will for my life. Paul encouraged us to "only let us live up to what we have already attained" (Phil. 3:16). God has spoken through his Word, and he continues to do so.

I encourage you to make your own list. Spend time reading through the Bible and writing down how you can implement what you read. When you go through a season of not knowing what God wants you to do, revisit your list and start doing what you've written down.

Hebrews 4:12 says that "the word of God is alive and active." This is one of the main ways (if not *the* way) God communicates to us—through the Scriptures. In them, God has laid out much of his will for our lives. You won't find a verse that tells you to move to Chicago instead of Denver. Nor will you find a verse that tells you to become an accountant instead of a teacher. But by being obedient to the broader commands of God, figuring out the specific callings will become easier. John wrote in his first epistle, "We know that we have come to know him if we keep his commands" (1 John 2:3). Our goal of discerning God's specific call on our lives starts with obedience to his call in Scripture.

WHERE DID THAT COME FROM?

Has God put something in your heart that pops up at random times? When I was in college, I kept hearing about Africa. The thought of Africa came up a lot. During prayer times or when reading the Bible, Africa would peek her head in. During class, I'd find myself thinking about Africa—*What is it like? Why do I keep thinking about it? Should I go there?*

After a few weeks, I couldn't shake the thought of Africa, so I bought a map of Africa and hung it in my room next to my desk. I wasn't sure why the thought kept coming up, but I was going to do my best to find out. Every day I'd look at the map and ponder Africa. When January rolled around, I had no resolution about Africa. There had been no more clues. I was certain it wasn't Professor Plum in the library with the candlestick, but that was about it.

"Why does it keep coming up?" I asked Betsey.

"Do you think you're supposed to go there?"

"I'm not sure. I don't know anyone in Africa. Actually, I don't even know anyone who's been there."

"Why don't you start there?" Betsey asked. "Let's look into some ways you could go. Maybe a short-term mission trip."

"That's a good idea."

That semester, I took a South African history class, which would further develop the nudges. For the class, we read *Long Walk to Freedom*, the autobiography of Nelson Mandela. I was captivated as he described the beauty of the country, but also the pain that its people had endured. Suddenly, the nudges became clear. I was supposed to go to South Africa. The only problem was that I didn't know anyone in South Africa. So, I began my quest in the same way most ideas start for me: Google.

Over the course of a few weeks, I discovered a handful of ministries that were doing short-term mission work in South

Africa. I reached out to each of them via e-mail, hoping to get some more information and inquire about the possibility of my going with them that summer.

Of those I e-mailed, I only heard back from one. This group was looking for a few college students to help facilitate short-term mission trips for high school students that coming summer. I printed off the application and sent it back within a few days.

God had opened a door that six months before I hadn't even known existed. I still had questions about how I was going to pay for it, as I would have to pay my own way and some expenses while I was there. My dad offered to give me some airline miles to help pay for the sixteen-hour flight to Cape Town. Later in the semester, I found an unmarked envelope in my car with a wad of cash and a note that said, "Praying for you." I was overwhelmed with the provision of God once I accepted the call to go to South Africa. I spent the summer helping the missionaries in all areas of their ministry. We built a playground and helped clean up an orphanage for abandoned children. We spent time training local pastors. Multiple times a week we would go out to give food to specific families in need. I will never forget the look on one mother's face when we stopped by to visit with her. I'm sure I was more impacted in the moment than she was. And I agree with Mandela—the country was absolutely beautiful. Cape Town remains one of my favorite cities in the world.

So what do you do if God nudges you with a random thought, like my thoughts of Africa? Or maybe for you it's Ohio, orphans, or the local school system. Your first step should be to acknowledge to God that you are aware of the nudge. Next, commit that you won't pray about action once you're called to act, but that you'll willingly act right away. After that, pray about what the nudge means. At the same time, though, begin your investigation. If it's a local area, spend some time driving around. If it's a friend or estranged family member, give them a call or write a letter to see how they're doing. Ask your friends if they know anything about the topic. Spend some time online. Maybe watch a documentary.

Finally, when an opportunity comes up for you to act on the nudge, do it. Immediately. Without hesitation. If God nudges you to be more generous with your money, then next time you see a need, meet it. If missions keep coming up, sign up for the next trip. If it's about going back to school, fill out the application. Whatever the nudge is, find ways to act as opportunities arise.

Sometimes the nudge will be a simple task that will have minimal effect past your current day. Other times, the nudge will be like a domino that sets in motion a series of events that alter the trajectory of your life.

CHAPTER 14

MY "STOP-PRAYING, START-DOING" OPPORTUNITY

I WAS SITTING ALONE IN THE BACK OF AN AUDITORIUM DURING a worship set at a conference I was attending in Chicago when I heard something. It shook me to my core. In a second, everything changed. Everything I'd been praying about. Everything I'd been working on. Everything I thought I understood about what God was doing changed. In a quiet moment of worship, I heard God speak to me. The music was loud, but I know what I heard. It wasn't an audible voice. A man in a white suit with the voice of Morgan Freeman didn't deliver a message to me, but I'm certain God spoke to me. It was a quiet nudge. The only thing I heard was: *Walk away from Backstage Leadership.*

My heart doubled its rhythm in my chest as I began to process what I had heard. *There's no way,* I kept telling myself. *There are many things I know God wants me to do, but certainly this is not one of them.*

For years, I had been trying to follow the leading of God

135

for my career and family. I didn't want to be another family man who worked a nine-to-five schedule, worked hard for the next promotion, put a little money in a 401(k), took two weeks of vacation, and continued until retirement. I wanted ours to be a family that listened to God and did what he said, no matter what. If God called us, I wanted to follow with obedience.

So, it shouldn't have been too surprising when an opportunity to be obedient came quietly knocking on the door. For a few months, I had been working with the idea for this book. I couldn't shake the thought of how often we settled for prayer when God wanted us to act. Whether God was trying to be funny or merely testing the depth of my conviction, I do not know; but during the middle of working on this book I knew he wanted me to stop praying and start doing. I've wondered what God may have called me to do had I instead been working on a book called *How to Spend a Million Dollars When a Distant Relative Leaves You His Inheritance*. I guess I'll never know.

I'd poured my life into this ministry over the past few years. Our family had sacrificed so much. There were months with no salary and months of praying that enough donations would come in to pay the bills. For years we planned, prayed, and lived with little margin to see Backstage Leadership succeed. Just the night before, we had hosted an event that was a raving success. The ministry was finally working. We were in the black on the income statements. We were sustaining and growing. But I knew what I had heard: *Walk away from Backstage Leadership.*

THE BEGINNING

Backstage Leadership was a ministry I'd started three years earlier after a series of events led me to believe God had opened a door and was leading me through it. Two years before, with the help of my wife, brother, and a few close friends, we started a nonprofit ministry. This was one of the first "stop-praying, start-doing" moments of my life. After learning that an estimated twenty-seven million people live in slavery in our world today, I knew we needed to do something. I didn't let the fact that I had zero experience in the nonprofit world, or in the social-justice world, slow us down. I wanted to make a difference. As the vision of this organization began to take shape, it became evident that I should assume the leadership role. Over the course of the next year, I devoted more and more time to seeing the vision come to reality.

The first major initiative was a complete flop—and I mean a complete and utter flop. Months of work and fund-raising amounted to next to nothing. I had taken four months away from my sales job to work ("volunteer" would be a more accurate description) full-time on the initiative. Our idea was taking longer and costing more than originally planned. Finally, a decision was made that we needed to scrap everything and go in a different direction. That was a painful decision. Knowing what I know now, I look back and laugh, wondering what we were thinking. But I also look back with gratefulness, knowing that God was using that time to open a new door. We had failed, or so it seemed.

After regrouping, we decided to focus our efforts in a very

specific way to help a small number of modern-day slaves with a project called Free Chains. If you want to help the twenty-seven million, you start by helping one. So that's what we did. Our organization partnered with a small ministry in Katmandu, Nepal, that was fighting to stop human trafficking in one of the poorest countries in the world. We focused our efforts on raising support for this incredible ministry, and we began to see God's blessing. I started speaking at churches, events, and for any audience that would have me, telling them of the incredible injustice that was going on in the world and offering a way they could help. I once used a business networking lunch to talk about modern-day slavery instead of my sales job. There were more than a few confused attendees! In less than a year's time, we raised enough money to support a bold plan to build and staff a border patrol station on the Nepal-India border. We later learned that in the two years following our support hundreds of women and children were rescued before they were trafficked out of the country into lives of slavery. I'm grateful we didn't give up.

WHO'S GOT TALENT?

When we're faithful with what God has given us, he promises to give us more. I don't know the exact formula, or even if there is one, but God said that the faithful will be given more. In the gospel of Matthew, Jesus tells a parable about three servants who were trusted by their master with a different amount of talents—that is, money. One was given five, one two, and the last servant was given one talent. Jesus said that the differing amounts were due to the ability of each servant. After giving the talents, the master went away on a journey.

Each of us is like one of the servants. We have been entrusted by God with varying levels of talents, which stretch far past money alone. You may have athletic, business, or musical talent. Some of you have been entrusted with the talent to lead, preach, or speak different languages. Your talent may be cooking, writing, or performing surgery. Or like the servants in the parable, you may have bags of gold, and how you invest your talent is of vast importance to God. "The man who had received five bags of gold went at once and put his money to work and gained five bags more" (Matt. 25:16).

Here, the emphasis on time is important. The man who received the most—which also means he had the most to lose—put his money to work "at once." He didn't wait to time the market just right.

One of the reasons we wait around before acting when God has called us is our failure to grasp the gravity of timing. The master didn't tell any of the servants when he would return from his journey. The man who was given five bags of gold realized that his master could be back from his journey the day after next. Even if he only had a few days, he knew the master would still require a return on the investment he'd left with the servant. So he got to work. The servant who was given two bags of gold did the same. He immediately put his gold to work, knowing he would be held accountable for what he did with it.

The third servant did something very peculiar. Instead of putting his money to work, he did the modern equivalent of hiding his money under his mattress. "But the man who had received one bag went off, dug a hole in the ground and hid his master's money" (Matt. 25:18).

This servant was paralyzed by fear. Maybe he'd lost a fortune in the prehistoric dot-com crash or saw the tent market crash from shady bank loans. Either way, he was afraid of what the master would do to him if he lost any of the money. So instead of taking a risk, he buried it, thinking it would be better to get zero return than to invest it and lose.

I think the third servant was aware that the other servants had received more than he did, and this birthed the internal conversations of doubt. The voices began talking to him: *You're not good enough. You only received one bag. You can't do anything great with just one bag. You may as well forget about it.*

This is what happens when we play the comparison game. We get sucked into focusing on what we don't have instead of maximizing what we do have. This servant failed to realize that he had a bag of gold! How many servants in his day would have had a piece of gold, much less a bag of it?

How many people around the world would look at your life and say, "He's got five bags and I only have one"? Most likely, if you are reading this book, you live in a fully developed world. You received a great education. You have plenty of food to eat. You have enough spare time to read a book because you don't have to walk for hours each day to get clean water—the way millions of people do every day. The truth is, you have been given five bags, and much will be expected of you.

I think this parable teaches some great lessons for us today. First, it shows us that we all have been given talents. Every one of us has something we can leverage for the glory of God.

Second, we see that not all talents are equal. Some have been given more than others. For those of you who have been given more, more will be expected of you. Third, we see that even if you've been given less, something is still expected. You do not get a pass. You will not be rewarded for burying your talent in the sand, hoping not to mess anything up. You are still expected to invest what you've been given.

Which servant in the parable do you connect with the most? Do you readily and quickly invest the talents with which you've been entrusted? Or do you bury what you've been given because you think it's not worth much? Take an honest assessment of what you've been given and determine how you are leveraging it for God's kingdom. And I want you to compare the results not just with those in your neighborhood, church, or office; compare them with around the world and then reevaluate your conclusion.

A GIFT FROM THE SKY

As I was developing my nonprofit ministry and growing the Free Chains project, I began developing a number of new friendships with people who had similar dreams and passions. I met people who wanted to change the world, and they were taking risks to do it. I met people starting nonprofits to serve the poor in Burma. There were guys starting clothing companies to fund clean water projects. There were women opening safe houses in major cities for rescued trafficking survivors.

I met people who were starting conferences to gather all

these like-minded people together. After many hours of conversations, I noticed some common themes in all the discussions. I could predict with incredible accuracy the answers many of these people would give to questions like:

- How are things going?
- How is fund-raising coming?
- How are things at home?
- What's the biggest challenge you're facing right now?

After a while, it felt like I was having a conversation with myself. I knew exactly how things were going with them because I was going through the same things. I knew how fund-raising was because I was in the middle of fund-raising. I knew their challenges at home because I was having the same ones. I knew the ups and downs, wins and losses.

But there was a big difference between where our team was and where these new friends were. We were overcoming some major obstacles. We were raising money. Relational landmines were being addressed. While we were going through the same struggles, God had blessed our team with some incredible mentors and leaders to help navigate the path we were traveling. These men and women had already walked down the difficult path we were on, and their advice helped push us through the most difficult problems.

As I was reflecting one day on the ministry and where we were going, all this came to focus in my mind. So much of our success was due to our connections with those who had gone before us—to their wisdom, experience, and advice. Were it not for their timely advice, I believe we would have been stuck in the same place as many of my new friends. Therefore, if intersecting with people who had already walked our path was the biggest factor in separating success from failure, then by working to create those intersection moments we could influence hundreds of leaders who would then go on to influence tens of thousands more.

I came home and shared five of the scariest words with my wife: "Oh, I have an idea." And with that, Backstage Leadership was born.

Of course, an idea is nothing more than an idea when it's only in your head, so I set out to bring Backstage Leadership to life. All I had to do was raise more money, on top of our Free Chains budget. For one, I had to build a new website. More important, I had to convince the mentors I knew to participate in intersection moments with young leaders who weren't currently signed up because they'd never heard of the idea in my head called Backstage Leadership. It sounded daunting, but I wasn't deterred.

After discussing the idea with my close friends and our ministry's board of directors, I was convinced that we were onto something special. We prayerfully considered what this would mean for my time and for our current ministry obligations. After feeling confident in prayer that I should pursue this, I immediately set out to work. I want to note that I felt confident we had a good idea and it should be pursued. This came through praying and seeking wise counsel. Prayer gave me the peace to move forward; that was it. I did not say amen from our prayer time and then, lo and behold, there was a detailed plan with step-by-step instructions from God in my inbox. There was no immediate phone call from a long-lost uncle who was leaving our ministry an endowment that would fund everything.

Prayer did not produce the immediate signs that so many people require from God before moving forward in faith. We want the instruction manual, because once we have that we can get to work. If that's what you're waiting for, you will most likely be waiting for a while. Aren't you glad that Peter didn't wait for God to send him *10 Easy Steps to Planting the First Church* before he got started on building the first church? He knew Jesus had called him to lead the first church, but as far as we know there was no instruction manual.

GET TO WORK

Having no instruction manual myself, I decided the best thing to do was start making phone calls. I had a clear vision, but if no one sees your vision, no one will be moved. Visions shared are the only ones capable of moving people to action.

So I started sharing my vision. Our leadership team began organizing how Backstage Leadership would work, what we would offer, and the details we needed to think of to roll out the new ministry. Our biggest obstacle was securing speakers—but not just *any* speakers. We needed great leaders and influencers whom young leaders would want to intersect with. These young people would need to connect with those who had successfully navigated the same scenarios they faced. But the issue with getting great speakers was the lack of participants.

The first questions speakers usually ask are about the audience. Who's going to be there? What type of leader is participating? How large is the audience? Of course, at this point we had no audience. I was trapped in the proverbial chicken-or-the-egg scenario. I couldn't get one without the other.

But one phone call changed all that.

I had a list of almost a hundred potential speakers. After scanning the names, I started with a leader I'd had a few interactions with over the past few years. I shared the vision for what we wanted to do and before I'd even wrapped up the big ask, he said, "I'm in. How can I help?" I remember that moment like it was yesterday. I was pacing the length of the hallway between bedrooms in our house. I had so much adrenaline pumping that I couldn't keep still while sitting down, so I paced. When he said he was in, I wanted to let out a loud *Braveheart*-esque scream of excitement but didn't want to scare him off. I quickly thanked him and told him I'd be following up soon with actual logistics.

I'd been looking for that break, and I knew the dominoes would start to fall. The dominoes must have been set too far apart, however, because nothing else happened. No other dominoes fell. There was no chain reaction. There was no tipping point. It was one and done. For months, I had one speaker, no participants, and no idea what to do next.

NEXT SCENE

One of the difficult aspects of reading the Scriptures is that months and years can go by in a story when we turn just one page. Take the story of the Old Testament patriarch Jacob, for instance. After deceiving his father and stealing from his brother, Esau, Jacob hit the road. A few sentences later, he was on the other side of the known world. In his travels, he came to Paddan Aram, the home of some distant relatives. As he approached his uncle Laban's estate, Jacob met Rachel, Laban's daughter. It was love at first sight. Many of you probably had the same experience when you met your future spouse:

> When Jacob saw Rachel daughter of his uncle Laban, and Laban's sheep, he went over and rolled the stone away from the mouth of the well and watered his uncle's sheep. Then Jacob kissed Rachel and began to weep aloud. (Gen. 29:10–11)

Apparently, there would be no date until the sheep had been watered, so Jacob lowered himself into the mud and got to work. When he finished, he kissed her. At this point, there had been no conversation—just watering sheep and kissing. (I told you this was probably just like your first date.) As if his first impression hadn't been strong enough, he started to sob. Not a little tear of joy rolling down his cheek, but an uncontrollable flood of emotion. He then let the cat out of the bag that they were cousins and she ran off to tell her father.

If I were Jacob, at this point I would be slightly concerned as I replayed the past few minutes (or hours?) in my head. *I'm exhausted from being on the run after stealing from my brother. I see a beautiful woman, and after watering her father's sheep I kiss her, explain we are cousins, start sobbing, and probably freak her out. Then she takes off running to her father. What have I done?*

First impressions are so important. Could Jacob possibly recover from this? Both Rachel and Laban were excited about the previous encounter, as the next verse explains: "As soon as Laban heard the news about Jacob, his sister's son, he hurried to meet him. He embraced him and kissed him and brought him to his home" (Gen. 29:13).

Laban then gave Jacob a place to stay and a job on the ranch.

By the next verse, an entire month had passed. Laban asked Jacob how he'd like to be paid. Can you imagine working for an entire month before bringing up the topic of a paycheck? Apparently, Jacob had been thinking about it a lot, as he knew exactly what he wanted. He wanted to marry Rachel, the younger of Laban's two daughters.

What's shocking to me is his lack of negotiating skills in this transaction. He was able to swindle his older brother twice, first by getting the birthright and then by receiving his father's blessing, both of which should have been his brother's. Jacob was sly. He knew how to get what he wanted. Apparently, love *is* blind, because he started the bidding so high that Laban didn't even need to respond. Jacob said, "I'll work for you seven years in return for your younger daughter Rachel" (Gen. 29:18). Seven years? Why not start with one year, or three? Why did he go straight to seven? These are not eBay rules, where the highest bid number will be accepted.

Just one verse separates the transaction with the payout: "So Jacob served seven years to get Rachel, but they seemed like only a few days to him because of his love for her" (Gen. 29:20).

One verse envelops seven years of working on a ranch in the Middle East. This is seven years of hard labor, early mornings, hot days, long hours, cold nights, herding cattle, wading through animal feces, all while being so close to your future wife, but not being able to be alone with her. Those were seven long years, all crammed into one verse.

As it turns out, the swindler had become the swindlee. On Jacob's wedding night, after Jacob had waited seven years to marry Rachel, Laban secretly slipped Leah, the uglier, older daughter, into Jacob's tent.

Jacob was shocked to find out he had actually married Leah instead of Rachel and went to settle the matter with Laban. Apparently the number seven was stuck in Jacob's head, and he had not learned to negotiate any better than the last time, so he promised to work another seven years if Laban promised to let him marry Rachel. Laban agreed and Jacob started out on another seven-year work detail that passed in only a few short verses.

In the matter of a chapter, we see fourteen years of Jacob's life. No details are given or other interactions with God mentioned. When things didn't go right, we don't hear a word from the Lord. Jacob just kept his head down and kept working, the way he felt God wanted him to do. Many times we are walking down a path we feel certain God called us to, only to enter a time of uncertainty. It seems nothing happens for days; days turn into weeks; weeks turn into months; and then sometimes months turn into years. During times like these, we all experience doubt. *Am I doing the right thing? It seemed right at first, but is this still what God has for me? Am I qualified for this? What was I thinking? This will never work.*

The longer we have to wait, the louder the voices get. And

here's the thing about the voices: they always have a kernel of truth in their statements. Even if it's a tiny fraction of a percent of truth, we get fixated on it, and many times it locks us down. Doubt grows into fear, which leads to inaction, which leads to a subtle death of obeying the call we received from God. What can we do during these times of doubt and uncertainty?

What did Jacob do during the seven years crammed into one verse? He kept working. That's all we can assume based upon what we know. Most likely, he did other activities besides work. But we know for certain that he kept working for Laban. His deal was simple—get Rachel and in return work for seven more years. Within a few verses of this deal, Jacob finally got Rachel as his wife, so we know he fulfilled his end of the bargain. For seven years, he kept working the daily grind—early mornings, late nights, and long days. Because he was dialed in to what he was working for, the seven years seemed like days. Maybe that's why they only got one verse.

There will be times when there is nothing in front of us but work. Many times this will not be the glamorous work that makes the front-page news, but rather the menial work that few will ever notice. When the voices of fear and doubt grow louder, you must continue to be a proactive pray-er. Listen to the voice of truth and know that God has a plan for all the work you are doing. When the days turn into years, know that you are potentially one phone call away from everything changing. That is exactly what happened to me in the struggle to get Backstage Leadership off the ground.

CHAPTER 15

ONE LAST SHOT

THE DAYS STRETCHED TO WEEKS, AND THE WEEKS TO MONTHS.
After months of work, I still only had one speaker for Backstage
Leadership, no participants, and nothing promising on the
horizon. The voices of doubt weren't whispering now; they had
taken up full-time residency and were making themselves welcome in all my thoughts. They were shouting. They were like
the heckler at a comedy act.

But there were other thoughts besides doubt and fear. There
was the smaller voice of persistence that pushed me to keep
going. There was the voice of encouragement that reminded me
there were people who needed this ministry. Then there was the
voice that reminded me to remain confident in God's call, since
nothing else had been spoken. If I had felt confident months
before that God wanted me to do this, why would I think that
had changed? I hadn't felt or heard anything different from God.
The only thing that had changed was my encounter with the real
world. True, things weren't going exactly as planned, but should

that have stopped me from staying on the path? It didn't stop Jacob. So I kept working, and something incredible happened.

Over the Christmas holidays, I was reading a book about boldly pursuing God's will for your life. I was still very much wrestling with why I was gaining no traction with Backstage Leadership. One idea from the book gripped my heart and wouldn't let go. The author asked how we would feel if we gave up on a dream, only to find out later that the break we needed was coming the very next day. Whether meaning to or not, the author scared me into working for one more day. I just had to find out what would happen. I couldn't cut off the movie before I found out what happened to the main character. Tomorrow was enough to keep me going today.

I made one more phone call that day. That phone call led to a lunch, which led to an e-mail, which led to the author of that very book committing to speak for Backstage Leadership. That speaker led to another call, which led to another speaker. In a matter of weeks we had a roster of speakers consisting of *New York Times* best-selling authors, mega-church pastors, billion-dollar business owners, and leaders who had spent time with the president of the United States. All because of one more phone call.

The reality is that it was more than one phone call. It was the cumulative effort of years of work, but all would have been for naught if I hadn't made that one call. What is your one more phone call? What is it that you need to keep doing, knowing it could be what sets in motion everything you've been striving for? You are potentially one decision away from all that you've been praying and working toward.

For the next few years, Backstage Leadership grew and

made an impact on many young leaders. The conversations between the speakers and participants were some of the richest learning moments of my life. Thankfully, many of the sessions were recorded, and I have often referred back to them to glean wisdom and experience. But the best part was forging new relationships with all the participants. I loved getting to know these church planters, business owners, entrepreneurs, artists, creative thinkers, and soon-to-be world-changers—and that would be the hardest part about walking away.

WALKING AWAY

After hosting an incredible Backstage Leadership event, dreaming about what was next, I found myself relaxing in the back of that worship service in Chicago, enjoying a time of stillness. The music in the room was loud, but the voice was crystal clear: *Walk away from Backstage Leadership.*

How could I possibly walk away? I think that was a very practical question. After all, I'd poured everything into building this ministry, even when it seemed that there was no chance of success. Lives were being changed. We were growing, and the finances were finally in the black. Did I mention I had a one-year-old and my wife was eight months pregnant at the time? How would I provide for my family? The small voice was clear, but all the other voices were screaming. And they were asking very good questions. I remember sitting there wanting to laugh and cry. There was nothing to do at that moment, so I just let it sit, unresolved, tension and all.

After I'd been home for a few days, I knew I needed to bring it up with my wife and team. I caught everyone up on Chicago and how the event had gone. Everyone was excited to hear about the continued success. Then I told them about what I felt God was telling me to do. What was interesting is that no one was shocked. Not one of my closest advisors told me it was a terrible idea. But they did ask realistic, logistical questions. There was a ministry that needed running. I had to help provide for my growing family. I went on to explain that I hadn't gotten that far in the conversation with God. I hadn't heard him say what was next. I hadn't heard him say what would happen to Backstage Leadership. All I'd heard was the call to walk away. That's all I knew to do.

Our leadership team decided to take six weeks to pray about the logistical unknowns. We would reconvene and make the wisest decision. We were not praying about whether or not I should walk away. Our prayers were focused on what to do with the ministry. We felt we were stewards of a ministry God had given us, and we wanted to handle it with great care. Our prayers were focused on what it meant for the ministry for me to walk away. Six weeks came and went, and the only answer I had for the team was that I was still supposed to walk away. There was no clarity on who should take my place and what would happen in the near future; I still only knew I was to walk away. So that's what I did. I stepped out of the day-to-day operations, and we hit the Pause button on Backstage Leadership. It was an incredibly difficult yet strangely peaceful decision. It was painful to walk away from something I'd helped build from scratch, pouring into it years of work and prayer. But the peace I felt was that Philippians peace Paul wrote about. He wrote to his followers:

> Do not be anxious about anything, but in every situation, by prayer and petition, with thanksgiving, present your requests to God. And the peace of God, which transcends all understanding, will guard your hearts and your minds in Christ Jesus. (Phil. 4:6–7)

I didn't have an understanding of all that was going on. I had no idea why I was walking away. I had no idea what was next. But through prayer and petition God gave me a peace that made me okay with not knowing all the answers. Our society doesn't deal well with not knowing all the answers. We are punished in school for not knowing the answers. We are expected to know where we want to go to college, what we'll major in, and what job we'll take after graduation. Our parents want to know what our next step will be and where we're going. Our in-laws want to know how we're going to provide for their sons and daughters. When we can't answer these questions, our culture demands an answer. If we can't answer them, we're labeled as lazy, ignorant, or foolish.

Ultimately, this is a collision of worldviews. The world says we should always know what's next. The Scriptures tell us that this won't always be the case. Sometimes we won't know. Sometimes God only gives us step one of a hundred-step plan, only to reveal step two once we've taken that first step, and not a second sooner. While that is a scary place to be, it is a beautiful place. In those moments we are able to declare with our actions that we trust that God is who he said he is and that he'll do what he promised he'd do. This is the determining factor in living a life fully committed to God. Do you trust him? If we trust him, we won't be anxious about anything, as Paul wrote. Instead of anxiety, we will have peace. How can that be?

That peace doesn't come through prayer alone. Millions of people pray every day, but I doubt they all feel the peace Paul described. I know I don't always have that peace. Then what's the secret? Where does the peace come from? The key is to notice the promise Paul made in the verse before he mentions the peace. He reminds his readers that "the Lord is near" (Phil. 4:5). In Greek this literally means that the Lord is "at hand." Paul wanted his readers to know that whatever they were going through, they were not alone, for Jesus was with them—he was near.

When we let the totality of that truth sink in, our view completely changes. The young girl is no longer afraid of the dark when her father comes into the room and holds her because he possesses strength greater than hers. She knows he provides a level of protection beyond her own capabilities. He is able to break her fear of the dark by entering it with her, then reassuring her with his continued presence. While she could probably never fully explain why, she has peace because her father is near.

NOTHING

The next few months brought no revelations, no breakthroughs, and no road maps. Backstage Leadership had officially been put on hold, and I was no closer to understanding why I was supposed to walk away. Around this time, I followed up with a friend who had worked for International Justice Mission, an incredible organization I had followed for years. I shared briefly about some of the areas of ministry I was hoping to get back into—including college ministry and preaching. I had felt called to preach years ago, and over the years had taken as many opportunities as possible. Many asked why I didn't plant a church. Considering that I love preaching, leadership, and starting things, it did seem like a good possibility. But I had never felt that the timing was right.

My friend explained that a position to help lead their college team was opening up soon and I should consider applying. As a former college pastor, the thought of getting back into college ministry was something I had been thinking about. The job would include public speaking, which I love. It would also include helping start new initiatives, which excited the entrepreneur in me. Add to that the overall mission of the organization—justice, which was a growing passion—and the job sounded incredible, almost too good to be true. I couldn't help but wonder if this was the reason I had walked away.

I told my wife about the job, and we both thought it could be a great opportunity. All I knew was that the job would be listed soon. My only option was to check their website for job openings and apply when I saw the opening posted.

As with Jacob's story, I only need one sentence to say that nothing changed in two months. Then the day came when the job opening was posted on the website. I was ready to go with my application, and I have to believe I was the first person to apply for the position. Within a few weeks, I was setting up a phone interview and finally moving forward with the process.

Then something unexpected happened. A few weeks after the phone interview, I received a call thanking me for applying, but I would not be hired after all.

WALKING THROUGH CLOSED DOORS

One of the dangers of trying to connect the dots for God is that sometimes one of the dots will suddenly vanish. It seemed so obvious that God was leading me to walk through this door. Now the door was closed, and the job was no longer an option. It was time to move on. Or was it?

Before Jesus died and rose from the dead, he showed his followers that he had the power to overcome death. As humans, our natural tendency is to focus on the closed door, to stare at death, making it difficult to see an alternative. God is in the business of opening closed doors and bringing what is dead back to life.

Jesus was preaching one day when a message arrived that Lazarus, his dear friend, was sick. Jesus was not surprised by this news, as the first words out of his mouth were, "This sickness will not end in death" (John 11:4). He knew exactly what Lazarus's sisters were concerned with: death. Lazarus was dying. To everyone, the dots were being connected into what was obviously death. Jesus tried to encourage them that this would not be Lazarus's fate because Jesus knew them and loved them. But Mary and Martha had connected the dots for themselves. Lazarus was sick and was obviously dying. They believed Jesus had the power to prevent his death. The critical dot to be connected was that Jesus needed to come immediately.

Jesus then did something completely unexpected. "So when he heard that Lazarus was sick, he stayed where he was two more days" (John 11:6).

I know how confused I got when I read that for the first time. Can you imagine what those with Jesus thought? The logical next step was for Jesus to run to Lazarus and heal him. If Jesus really loved Lazarus, why would he take so long? Why would he wait two more days? Now imagine what Mary and Martha were thinking. They were not with Jesus. They waited with their brother on his deathbed and sent someone to find Jesus, only to watch the hours and then days go by with no sign of Jesus.

By the time Jesus showed up, Lazarus had been in the tomb for four days. They'd already had the funeral. The tomb was sealed with a giant rock. This story was over, or so they thought.

When Martha heard Jesus was finally on his way, she ran to meet him outside the village. The first words out of her mouth were about connecting the dots: "Lord . . . if you had been here, my brother would not have died" (John 11:21). In other words, "Jesus, there was an obvious and easy plan, so why did you take so long? All this could have been avoided if you had shown up on time." Jesus then plainly told her, "Your brother will rise again" (John 11:23).

With that, one would think that Jesus had settled the issue. He hadn't been there when Martha thought he should have been, but he was ultimately going to give her what she wanted.

A few minutes later, a frustrated Mary showed up with the same point as Martha.

> When Mary reached the place where Jesus was and saw him, she fell at his feet and said, "Lord, if you had been here, my brother would not have died." (John 11:32)

When it comes to understanding the difficult situations in our lives, it is natural to focus on the ifs. *If I had only gotten that job. If she had shown up earlier. If only he had missed that flight.* We play out alternative outcomes in our minds, focusing on what could have been *if* something else had happened. We do this when the dots don't get connected the way we think they should. But in these moments God wants to teach us to trust him. Because even when we don't understand what God is doing, he is still working. He always has a plan, and his plan is always for the best.

After everyone, including Jesus, wept at the grave, Jesus ordered the stone to be rolled away. Martha, the practical one in the group said, "But, Lord, . . . by this time there is a bad odor, for he has been there four days" (John 11:39). She was worried about the temporal and practical.

Jesus, however, was clearly concerned with an entirely different realm. "Then Jesus said, 'Did I not tell you that if you believe, you will see the glory of God?'" (John 11:40).

Jesus was concerned not only with Lazarus; he loved all those there so much that he wanted them to experience the glory of God. Above all your circumstances, God is concerned with an additional realm. He cares about the immediate, but he also wants you to experience the glory of God.

> So they took away the stone. Then Jesus looked up and said, "Father, I thank you that you have heard me. I knew that you always hear me, but I said this for the benefit of the people standing here, that they may believe that you sent me." (John 11:41–42)

As Jesus prayed aloud, it became obvious to those listening that this whole situation had been much bigger than just preventing Lazarus from dying. Jesus loved Mary and Martha more than they had realized. He'd wanted them to experience a depth of faith that was only possible by going through a period of pain and uncertainty. To experience the joy of resurrection, you must endure the pain of death. Jesus called Lazarus by name, and Lazarus walked out of the tomb.

Preventing death is an incredible memory, but overcoming death is an unforgettable miracle.

NO RANDOM MOMENTS

There are no surprises in God's economy. God isn't shocked, spooked, or taken by surprise by anything that happens in the world. With God, there are no random moments. Four months after the job I applied for fell through, I was down to the last day to decide whether I should attend a conference in Washington,

DC. I'd loved attending this conference in the past, but it was a substantial cost, which had me second-guessing myself. I was trying to save as much money as possible to pursue a new ministry opportunity. After spending weeks asking my own "if" questions, I had admitted the job was dead and moved on. At the last moment, I purchased a flight to DC and attended the conference. The string of events that followed is nothing short of comical now.

As the conference broke for lunch on the first day, I ran into my friend who works for IJM, the organization I'd applied to work with. We talked about how bummed we both were that I hadn't gotten the job. I told her I had worked through it, but was now pursuing a new opportunity and felt very good about it. On our way to lunch, two of her colleagues joined us. One of them happened to be the woman who would have been my boss had I gotten the job the year before. As we were talking, I told her about my background and why I had originally applied for the job. I then went on to tell her about the new opportunity I was pursuing. As if I needed another reminder, I was once again reminded that the job was dead in the grave. She then said, "You really have a passion for all of this. It was great talking with you. Please stay in touch." Then came the nail in the coffin: "The gentleman we hired starts next Monday." Listen carefully and you can hear the hearse backing up.

While we were walking back to the conference, I couldn't help but laugh thinking about the exchange. As if I wasn't fully aware the opportunity was buried six feet under, God had brought one last reminder. We exchanged business cards, and I let her know I'd still love to help in any way. I honestly thought that would be my last encounter with IJM, and I was excited to move forward.

Lazarus spent four days in the tomb before Jesus raised him from the dead. When he walked out of the tomb, he was covered in grave cloths, showing that his sisters hadn't expected Jesus to resurrect him anytime soon. Jesus surprised them all when he called Lazarus out of the grave.

A few weeks after returning from DC, something interesting happened that surprised me too. I discovered that the job I'd applied for at IJM had become available again. Just when I thought I had figured out what God was doing, he went and did something like this. The stone was starting to roll away.

Intrigued, I decided to find out more. The next thing I realized, I was conducting a phone interview for the very job that weeks earlier had been dead to me. How could this be? Due to some personal reasons, the man who previously accepted the position had to politely decline at the last moment. I didn't ask any further questions about him, hoping everything was okay.

God is a God of bringing dead things to life. Within the next few weeks, I had conducted multiple phone interviews and was in the process of booking flights to DC for final interviews. When I was offered the job a few weeks later, all the thoughts and emotions of the past year flooded my mind. This was a job I had wanted, applied for, and then been denied. The job had been dead, but God resurrected it.

I learned many lessons through the entire process. One, don't start writing a book telling people God wants them to stop praying and start doing and not expect God to give an immediate opportunity to apply it. More important, I learned that God is able to bring anything back to life. Whether it's a job, a marriage, a parent-child relationship, a childhood passion, or a calling, God can bring it back to life. Even when we think there's no hope, life is possible. When we think all is lost, it's still possible. When the job is given to someone else, it's still not over until God says it is.

Whatever God is calling you to stop praying about and start doing, don't lose hope, even if all hope is lost. God is in the business of resurrecting what is dead and bringing it back to life.

WAITING FOR THE MIRACLE

The encounter Peter had with Jesus at the Sea of Galilee set in motion events that are still affecting people today. I want to look at the encounter and discuss a very important but often overlooked detail of the story told in Luke 5. The reason Peter decided to follow Jesus was the miracle Jesus had performed that morning. Peter had been fishing for most of his life, and he'd never experienced anything like that miracle. After following through on Jesus' advice to try fishing in the deep water, Peter and his crew caught so many fish that their boat began to sink. This was truly a miraculous catch.

It's true that most of us want to experience a miracle like Peter and his friends experienced that day. We don't necessarily want a miraculous catch of fish, but we do want a huge catch of God's blessings. In our businesses, we want a huge catch of profit. In our churches, we want a huge catch of people. In our families, we want a huge catch of deep relational connections. In our parenting, we want a huge catch of trust with our children. We all want our own miraculous catch. The question is, how can we get it? The obvious component of the miraculous catch equation is Jesus. That doesn't come as a shock to anyone. Without Jesus, there would have been no miracle. But there's another component we need to consider.

First, let's recap what happened. Peter and his friends worked all night and caught nothing. The word used for work in Greek means to toil. Fishing was grueling physical labor, and Peter was tired from the long night. Jesus showed up in the morning and was encircled by a huge crowd listening to him preach. The crowds were getting so large that Jesus asked Peter to stop what he was doing and push his boat out from the shore so Jesus could use it as a floating pulpit. While Jesus was preaching, Peter returned to the difficult work of washing his fishing nets—the nets that had brought no bounty after a night of toiling. Then Jesus wrapped up his sermon and told Peter to let his nets down in the deep for a catch.

I've always wondered what it was Jesus was teaching the crowds at that moment. Was he teaching about faith or how to pray? What if he was teaching on trusting God or the power of the Father? Whatever the topic, the next scene with Peter is one of the all-time best sermon illustrations ever.

> When they had done so [let down the nets for a catch], they
> caught such a large number of fish that their nets began to

break. So they signaled their partners in the other boat to come and help them, and they came and filled both boats so full that they began to sink. (Luke 5:6–7)

I want to think Jesus was teaching about trusting God. Maybe he said something like, "And when you have faith, God will provide more than you thought possible. Watch this. Peter, let down your nets." Peter caught more fish in a few minutes than he did toiling through the night.

Without a doubt, this is an incredible story of God's power and his ability to perform miracles in our lives. This is what so many of us want. We pray for the miracle of forgiveness from the family we walked out on. We pray for the miracle of healing for the addiction in our lives. We pray for the miracle of reconciliation between siblings after decades of feuding. We pray for the miracle of purpose after making it to the top of every ladder we thought would bring fulfillment. We pray for the miracle, but why doesn't God do anything?

Oftentimes, God probably asks the same thing of us: *Why aren't they doing anything? Why doesn't he seek professional help? Why doesn't she humble herself and ask for forgiveness? Why doesn't he go on that mission trip his neighbor keeps asking about?* Many times the reason we fail to receive the miracle we long for is because we aren't doing our part.

The most overlooked part of the fishing story above comes at the beginning of Luke 5:6: "When they had done so . . ." The "so" is Peter putting the nets back in for a catch. The fish didn't jump in the boat. The nets didn't float over into the water. Peter had to carry the nets back into the boat, row the boat out to the deep water where Jesus had told him to fish, lift the nets over the edge, drop them in the water, then pull the nets loaded with fish back into the boat with his hands. Remember, this was toil. This was grueling work. This was not a five-second miracle. It took time and physical effort by Peter and his companions.

Between Jesus' command and the miraculous catch was Peter's work. Peter had a role to play. Had he not done it, there would have been no miracle. Throughout history, God has continually used people to fulfill his will. Sure, there are times when God just acts, but historically people are his instruments of choice. He chose Joseph to be the instrument to save Jacob's family (and the entire known world) from a famine. God chose Noah to build a boat to preserve the human race from the coming flood. Ever wonder why God didn't just leave a completed boat in Noah's front yard? God chose Moses to lead the Israelites out of Egypt. When God wanted a church built and the gospel spread, he sent Peter and Paul on the road. God likes to use people to accomplish his will, and this includes miracles. Each of these characters had a role to play. God has his role, but he expects us to play ours as well.

There is one more thought to consider from this passage before we move on. It is possible to work incredibly hard and in the end have nothing to show for it. Peter worked hard all night, but it just wasn't his night. There is always the chance that we will do the work and get no return. There's a chance she won't forgive you. There's a chance you'll start the orphanage and get no supporters the first time you ask. There's a chance your nets will come up empty. Wilberforce came up empty nineteen years in a row before he saw the slave trade abolished in Great Britain. The key is to keep trusting the One who called you. Do not let the empty net allow you to quit what God has called you to do. If it comes up empty, keep going, for he called you to be obedient, and leave the results to him.

CHAPTER 16
YOU'LL NEVER KNOW UNLESS YOU GO

DURING MY JUNIOR YEAR IN COLLEGE, MY ROOMMATE AND I had a crazy idea. We discovered that it was possible to take summer classes at the University of Hawaii for six weeks, where we could live on campus and only have to pay in-state tuition. It would basically be the same cost as taking summer classes at our school, minus the cost of the flights. We looked at the university website and saw pictures of the beautiful island—the blue water, the lush mountains, the sandy beaches. Our plan was to take one or two morning classes so that we'd have the rest of the day to be college kids. Maybe we'd get part-time jobs at a resort or golf course. It was going to be the best summer ever. How could it not? Can you imagine spending six weeks in Hawaii and it not being fun?

But really I could only guess. I don't know what six weeks in Hawaii is like. I don't know what it's like to learn to surf. I don't know how great it is to watch the sunset over the North Shore or the sunrise over Waikiki. I don't know because we didn't actually do it. We never went. We missed registration, and we never followed up like we should have. Instead of a chance of a lifetime, it's a regret from my past.

Although it would have been better to say I got to spend an entire summer in Hawaii, I did at least learn a good lesson. I learned this principle: you'll never know unless you go. The only way I can understand what living in Hawaii for six weeks is like is to live in Hawaii for six weeks. But I missed my chance.

ALTERNATE ENDING

If Peter had known the end of his life before he decided to follow Jesus, there's a high probability that Luke 5 would contain a very different story. After Jesus left the apostles, Peter went on to lead the New Testament church. On the altar call of his very first sermon, three thousand people were saved. The number of people being saved continued to increase by thousands, making Peter the leader of the first mega-church. Some of his letters even made it into the New Testament.

We would all agree that Peter did huge things for God. History tells us that Peter was crucified for his faith. When he wouldn't stop preaching in the name of Jesus, he was arrested and tortured. Upon learning he was going to be crucified, he requested to be hung upside down because he wasn't worthy to be crucified like his Savior. Had Peter known the ending, maybe he would have reconsidered Jesus' call to follow him. Luke 5 is when everything changed for Peter. And this encounter is loaded with meaning for us today. Recall his interaction with Jesus:

> One day as Jesus was standing by the Lake of Gennesaret, the people were crowding around him and listening to the word of God. He saw at the water's edge two boats, left there by the fishermen, who were washing their nets. He got into one of the boats, the one belonging to Simon, and asked him to put out a little from shore. Then he sat down and taught the people from the boat. (Luke 5:1–3)

Peter had a small yes moment. Small yeses seem rather insignificant. Honestly, anyone can fulfill a small yes. Small yeses aren't decisions that change the world. There was any number of fishermen who could have given Jesus a boat. There wasn't much risk in it for Peter. He even may have been annoyed that he lost the use of his boat for a while.

But Peter felt a nudge. He knew he was supposed to let Jesus borrow his boat. Because of this decision, Peter set in motion an adventure he couldn't have imagined. A key element to the small yes is that it gets us closer to Jesus. In Peter's case, it got him closer to Jesus physically so he could hear Jesus teach. When you commit to the small yes, you put yourself in proximity to Jesus, where you are able to experience a deeper calling. Jesus' next request would be more difficult than the first one. "When he had finished speaking, [Jesus] said to Simon, 'Put out into deep water, and let down the nets for a catch'" (Luke 5:4).

Letting Jesus borrow the boat while it was tied up on the

shore was one thing, but putting down the nets for a catch was just crazy. In those days, people fished at night with large nets. This wasn't one man in a lake with a trolling motor and a little Shimano reel. It took a crew to fish. Was Jesus really questioning Peter's knowledge of fishing? What did Jesus know about fishing anyway?

Peter might have said, "You don't fish in deep water, Jesus. And you don't fish during the day. You're a carpenter. You whittle things out of wood. I don't come into your shop and tell you to make a table with only two legs, do I?"

Since Jesus had been teaching, quite a crowd was gathered around Peter's boat. Besides that, all his crew and employees were there, including some family members. Jesus had raised the stakes. If this went poorly, Peter would be the laughingstock of the community. But Peter decided to act. The longer you wait in a situation like that, the louder the internal voices become. The best way to shut them up is to get a move on. "Simon answered, 'Master, we've worked hard all night and haven't caught anything. But because you say so, I will let down the nets'" (Luke 5:5). Translation: "Jesus, I don't think you really get fishing. We've put in a full workday without results. And now you want me to break every rule in the book and try again? Now? In front of all these people?" This is a slightly bigger yes, and Peter had no idea what hung in the balance. You'll never know unless you go. Well, look at what happens when God's faithfulness intersects with our obedience: "When they had done so [let down the nets], they caught such a large number of fish that their nets began to break" (Luke 5:6).

They had to call in help as the boats began to sink. If he had said no to Jesus about the boat, Peter would have missed out on the chance to experience a remarkable miracle. At this point, Peter realized that he'd stepped into something much larger than himself. Peter freaked out and did the only acceptable thing in that situation. He bowed to his knees and begged for mercy in the sight of Jesus. "Then Jesus said to Simon, 'Don't be afraid; from now on you will fish for people'" (Luke 5:10).

Mark 1:17 translates it this way: "Come, follow me . . . and I will send you out to fish for people."

This was no longer a small yes. This was a call to change the world. What I love about Luke's version is that Jesus acknowledges there will be reasons to fear. He doesn't ignore that. Fishing when you're not supposed to can be embarrassing. Moving across the country may seem foolish. Forgiving your dad for leaving or your mom for being an alcoholic isn't easy. It is difficult. Jesus accepts this. But the next part is what makes obedience possible. Jesus points out in the verse from Mark that he himself will be there to make him into a fisher of men. Peter will not be alone, for Jesus will be with him.

Jesus wants to get us to the place where we can accept a calling to change the world. This starts with a small yes and ends with a big yes. Jesus didn't ask Peter to die for him first (which he would eventually do); he asked Peter to borrow his boat, toss a net, and then follow him as a disciple. It started with a small yes.

Say yes to the small requests, and in time you'll be able to make the big yes.

NO PRAYER?

Notice what Peter didn't do in this story. I'm assuming you've picked up on what I'm about to say. Peter didn't stop to have a prayer meeting. There was no jumping into the prayer closet to consider what Jesus had just said. Peter didn't break out his journal and write a prayer poem as he contemplated what Jesus had called him to do. Peter didn't pray about following Jesus. He just did it.

Does that bother you? I know that when I read this story, I tense up a bit. Here we have this New Testament church leader who walked away from everything he owned, including his job, responsibilities, family, and everything he knew, to follow Jesus, and he didn't even offer up a token prayer? Like, "God, if you don't want me to go this way, then give me a flat tire." Peter didn't even give thirty seconds to prayer, let alone thirty minutes, hours, or days.

If I were to do that today, most people would consider me a horrible husband and father, right? Peter didn't even go home and discuss it with his wife. You would think that she'd want to know that the family budget was about to take a hit and that he'd only be around every few months for the next three years.

Isn't that reckless? I mean, where is the wisdom? Where is the counsel? Where is the godly advice? How could what Peter was doing be at all justified? How could Peter answer the call to follow Jesus in such a haphazard way? The reason Peter could say yes when Jesus called him to do something great was that Peter also answered yes when he was asked to do the mundane. He overcame procrastination with a small yes. When the stakes were raised, Peter knew he could trust the nudge and drop the nets. Peter would never know what might have been had he not dropped the nets and followed Jesus. The same is true for you. You'll never know unless you go.

DO WE REALLY WANT TO KNOW?

Besides the help-me-win-the-lottery prayer, I would guess that one of the top prayers God hears relates directly to people asking about his will for their lives. *Should I marry him? Should I take this job? Should I start this business? Should I go to this university or that one? Should we move? Should I go to law school or medical school? God, what is your will for my life? God, what does the future hold for me?*

I'll admit that I've frequently prayed these types of prayers; but the older I get, I'm not so sure I want the entire picture. I think I do, but as I look at Peter's life, the step-by-step process seems a little easier to handle.

Put yourself in Peter's shoes, and consider Jesus describing to you the next few years and decades of your life. If this was you, would you have dropped the nets and followed him? The script might have gone something like this:

> **JESUS:** Peter, leave your fishing career behind and follow me.
>
> **PETER:** Okay, Lord. What will I be doing?
>
> **JESUS:** We're going to walk from village to village telling stories, casting out demons, raising people from the dead.

PETER: That sounds fun. Anything else?

JESUS: We'll feed some folks. Maybe hang out with some tax collectors and sinners. We'll do some more walking.

PETER: How much more?

JESUS: A lot more. But, speaking of walking, I have a surprise for you.

PETER: What is it?

JESUS: You'll spend some time walking on water.

PETER: That sounds like something I'd do.

JESUS: Yeah, but then you get scared, start to drown, and I'll have to save you.

PETER: (silence)

JESUS: But don't worry. Later you'll try and redeem yourself by cutting off a guy's ear.

PETER: What?

JESUS: Yeah, then a few hours later you'll get scared of some servant girls while I'm getting beaten. You'll flat-out deny that you know me.

PETER: (silence)

JESUS: Then you'll watch me die.

PETER: This doesn't sound like much fun.

JESUS: Don't worry, I'll come back to life.

PETER: Phew.

JESUS: Then I'll appoint you the leader of the first church.

PETER: Now we're talking.

JESUS: You'll heal people and boldly proclaim who I am to the Jews.

PETER: That sounds awesome!

JESUS: Then you'll watch many friends be persecuted for their new faith. Several of them will die.

PETER: (gulp)

JESUS: Then you'll get to stand in front of the entire Sanhedrin and they'll try and talk you out of talking about me.

PETER: What will I do?

JESUS: You'll be thrown in prison.

PETER: Prison?

JESUS: Oh yeah. A few times, actually.

PETER: Then what?

JESUS: You'll write a few letters that people will read for thousands of years.

PETER: That's pretty cool.

JESUS: And do you want to know how it all ends for you?

PETER: I'm not so sure.

JESUS: You, Peter, will be . . . (drumroll) . . . crucified.

PETER: What?

JESUS: That's right. Just like me.

PETER: Seriously?

JESUS: Well, not exactly like me. You'll actually be crucified upside down.

PETER: (silence)

JESUS: You ready? Let's go make fishers of men.

If Peter had known that persecution and a premature death were on the horizon, would he have followed? Would you have gone? I'm not sure about Peter, but I'll admit that I would have seriously considered passing. Our basic instinct is self-preservation. There has to be a very strong override to that instinct to willingly walk toward imminent death. No one runs into a burning building just for fun. The only reason you run into a burning building is to save something—or, more likely, someone—so valuable that you would willingly give your life.

This is the beauty of the small yes. I think it's one of the ways God protects us. The small yes allows us to deepen our trust in the Father and his call. With each yes, we build a little more trust, gaining a little more confidence for what the next call may be. If God isn't giving you the entire picture, rest in the possibility that this is a grace allowing you to only focus on the step in front of you.

WHAT ARE YOU WAITING FOR?

It's time to act on what God has called you to do. Our faith is one of action. Prayer leads to following through with what God has said. Prayer leads to peace and reassurance that acting on God's calling will bring about the good that God desires.

Prayer should never be an obstacle to accomplishing what God has called you to do. If you're procrastinating, isolating yourself with prayer, or becoming prideful when God calls you to act, you need to stop praying and start doing. Change your prayer life to be proactive instead of reactive, and you'll find the strength to say yes.

Peter told the church to prepare for action. Prayer is a great way to prepare for action, but don't just settle for preparation. Act! In the same letter, Peter encouraged his readers:

> Live such good lives among the pagans that, though they accuse you of doing wrong, they may see your good deeds and glorify God on the day he visits us. (1 Peter 2:12)

Again, the call is action. Peter didn't command the people to pray among the pagans. He told them to live good lives. Good lives encompass good actions. It is impossible to live among people and not act.

Following Jesus has always been about action. If there's no action in your life, you aren't following Jesus. It's impossible to be a disciple and stay still. When Jesus called the disciples to follow him, they literally walked behind him. If they had stayed where they were, they wouldn't have become his disciples. Being a disciple, in essence, means acting.

Today is the day to stop praying about what God has called you to do and do it!

There are as many calls to action as there are people on the planet. Here is a short list of possibilities that God wants you to stop praying about and start doing. Just because your call isn't on this list doesn't mean you should pass on taking action. Some calls will be easier than others. Some calls will require a lot of strength. Others will require help from many people.

- Tithing 10 percent of my income.
- Seeking help for an addiction.

- Forgiving my father.
- Changing my major.
- Passing on a promotion.
- Calling my sibling.
- Selling my business.
- Moving to India.
- Telling my son that I'm sorry.
- Going on a diet.
- Admitting I was wrong.
- Selling the lake house.
- Joining a church.
- Getting baptized.
- Moving to the inner city.
- Becoming a teacher.
- Joining the lesser-known firm.
- Writing a book.
- Stopping the excuses for missing my kids' events.
- Coaching the team.
- Stopping gossiping.
- Trading in the car.
- Moving out.
- Moving back in.
- Forgiving my ex-spouse.
- Correcting the IRS form.
- Inviting *them* to the party.
- Homeschooling my kids.
- Going on the mission field.
- Sponsoring a child in poverty.

What does life look like when we stop praying about what God has told us to do? It looks like less procrastination and more yeses. It looks like less isolation and more connection. It looks like less pride and more selflessness. It looks more like discipleship than religion. It looks more like excitement than fear. It looks like what life *should* look like.

Stop praying.

Start doing.

NOTES

CHAPTER 5

1. James Strong, *Strong's Hebrew Dictionary of the Bible*, (New York City: BN Publishing, 2012), s.v. "laqach."

CHAPTER 10

1. Eric Metaxas, *Amazing Grace: William Wilberforce and the Heroic Campaign to End Slavery* (New York City: Harper Collins, 2007), 123.
2. Ibid., 123.
3. Phillip Freeman, *St. Patrick of Ireland: A Biography* (New York City: Simon & Schuster, 2005), 184.
4. "Saint Patrick," *Saint Isidore the Farmer: Roman Catholic Church*, accessed December 8, 2013, http://www.saintisidore .org/religious-info/st-patrick.htm.
5. Phillip Freeman, *St. Patrick of Ireland: A Biography* (New York City: Simon & Schuster, 2005), 184.

CHAPTER 11

1. Ernest Gordon, *To End All Wars* (Grand Rapids: Zondervan, 1963), 48.

NOTES

2. Ibid., 48.
3. Ibid., 51.
4. Ibid., 65.
5. Ibid., 73.
6. Ibid., 73–74.
7. Ibid., 105.
8. Ibid.

ACKNOWLEDGMENTS

I WANT TO THANK JESUS FOR BLESSING ME WITH FAR MORE than I deserve. His grace is an unbelievable gift that I am so grateful for.

I want to thank my beautiful wife, Betsey, who is always the biggest supporter of all my crazy ideas. Thanks for how you lead and the example you set. You amaze me.

I want to thank my kids, whom I love far more than they'll ever know. Being your dad is just awesome.

Thanks to Chris, Lee, Stephen, Wesley, and Sandy for letting me bounce enough ideas off you until we found a great one. I have an incredible inner circle.

Thanks to Mark Sweeney for being an incredible agent and a guide I could trust. Here's to many more.

Thanks to Joel Miller, Katherine Rowley, Kristen Parrish, and the incredible team at Thomas Nelson for making the message of the book come to life.

ACKNOWLEDGMENTS

I want to thank Mark Batterson for being a huge encouragement to me and wanting to see this book written.

Thanks to Mike Foster and Perry Noble for letting me share a piece of your story. I know it will inspire others like it did me.

Thanks to Tyler, Adam, Joey, Bar, and Dan for jumping off the bridge. Korey and Brett, wish you could have been there.

I want to thank Jennifer Schuchmann for all the encouragement to keep writing. It meant a lot coming from a professional.

I want to thank all my colleagues at IJM who are changing the world every single day. I am honored to work with true heroes.

ABOUT THE AUTHOR

GREG DARLEY IS A SOCIAL ENTREPRENEUR, SPEAKER, WRITER. In his role as Director of College Mobilization for International Justice Mission (IJM), he leads IJM's more than seventy-thousand college students on hundreds of campuses across the country to engage in the work of justice.

Before coming to IJM, Greg was founder and director of BackstageLeadership.org, a national Christian leadership training program connecting and equipping Christian leaders, church planters, and pastors.

He is a graduate of Clemson University and has earned a master's degree from Liberty Theological Seminary. He also is a graduate of BreakPoint's Centurion Program, a biblical worldview training program created by Chuck Colson. He lives outside Washington, DC, with his wife and two children. Reach Greg at www.gregdarley.com and @gregdarley on Twitter.